Unforgotten

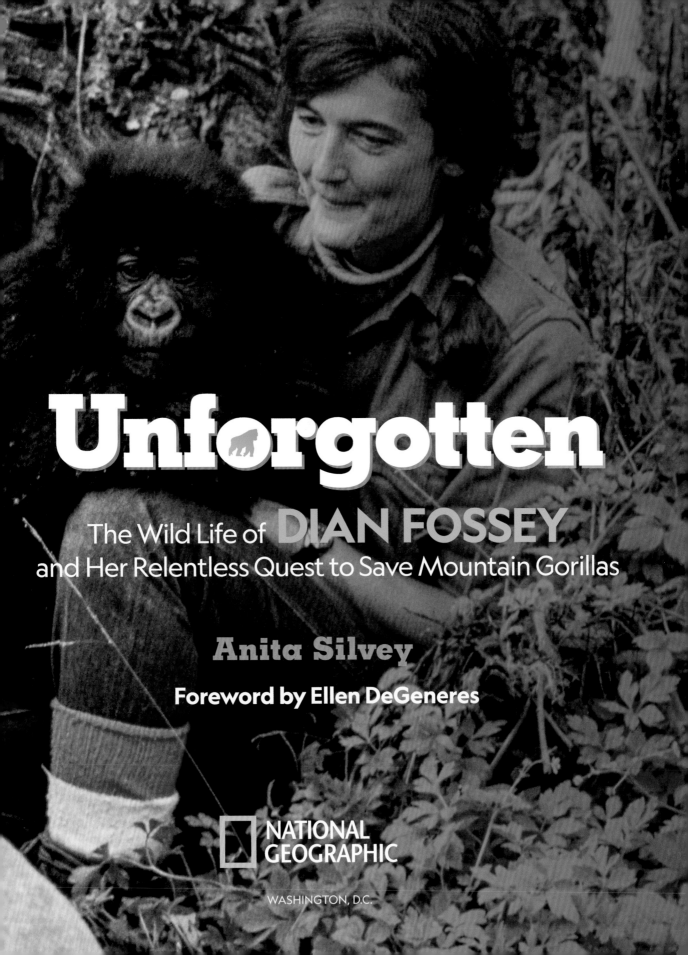

Unforgotten

The Wild Life of DIAN FOSSEY
and Her Relentless Quest to Save Mountain Gorillas

Anita Silvey

Foreword by Ellen DeGeneres

NATIONAL GEOGRAPHIC

WASHINGTON, D.C.

For Kate Hale, Editor Extraordinaire —AS

Since 1888, the National Geographic Society has funded more than 12,000 research, exploration, and preservation projects around the world. The Society receives funds from National Geographic Partners, LLC, funded in part by your purchase. A portion of the proceeds from this book supports this vital work. To learn more, visit natgeo.com/info.

For more information, visit nationalgeographic .com, call 1-877-873-6846, or write to the following address:

National Geographic Partners, LLC
1145 17th Street N.W.
Washington, DC 20036-4688 U.S.A.

For librarians and teachers: nationalgeographic .com/books/librarians-and-educators

More for kids from National Geographic: natgeokids.com

National Geographic Kids magazine inspires children to explore their world with fun yet educational articles on animals, science, nature, and more. Using fresh storytelling and amazing photography, *Nat Geo Kids* shows kids ages 6 to 14 the fascinating truth about the world— and why they should care.
kids.nationalgeographic.com/subscribe

For rights or permissions inquiries, please contact National Geographic Books Subsidiary Rights: bookrights@natgeo.com

Designed by Marty Ittner

The publisher and author would like to acknowledge and thank the dedicated staff at the Dian Fossey Gorilla Fund for their invaluable help with this project. Many thanks also to editor Erica Green, researchers Michelle Harris and Rose Davidson, photo editor Sarah Mock, and photo director Lori Epstein. Special thanks to Kate Hale.

FRONT COVER: Dian Fossey with orphaned mountain gorillas Coco and Pucker *(top)*; a baby mountain gorilla munching on bamboo *(bottom)*

BACK COVER: Dian with Coco and Pucker

CASE COVER: Silverback Cantsbee (far left) with some of the group he led, including his son, the young silverback Gicurasi (far right)

HALF-TITLE PAGE: A young mountain gorilla

TITLE PAGE: Dian Fossey with her dog, Cindy, and gorillas Coco and Pucker in Rwanda in 1969

CONTENTS PAGE: A 10-month-old mountain gorilla

Hardcover ISBN: 978-1-4263-7185-1
Reinforced library binding ISBN:
978-1-4263-7186-8

Printed in China
21/RRDH/1

Contents

Seeing mountain gorillas in Rwanda was a "dream come true" for Ellen DeGeneres and Portia de Rossi, who are supporting the Dian Fossey Gorilla Fund to build a campus there to carry on Dian's work of studying and protecting mountain gorillas.

Foreword

By Ellen DeGeneres

In January 1970, Dian Fossey was on the cover of *National Geographic*. I remember it because I was 12 years old and I had the cover of the magazine taped up on my bedroom wall. As a young girl, I loved animals and I loved nature. At a time when most kids were into the Beatles, I was into actual beetles.

I read the cover story over and over and over again until I had it memorized. Dian Fossey was living in Rwanda researching mountain gorillas, trying to save them from the brink of extinction. I was absolutely in awe. In fact, her work with the mountain gorillas is one of the things that inspired me to be an animal advocate.

Years later, for my 60th birthday, my wife, Portia de Rossi, got me the most extraordinary gift I have ever received: an 11-acre campus with my name on it at the Dian Fossey Gorilla Fund in Rwanda.

The goal of the Ellen DeGeneres Campus is to establish a permanent home for the Dian Fossey Gorilla Fund so that we can continue Dian's legacy of conservation. It will be a state-of-the-art, sustainably built destination for tourists, local Rwandans, scientists, students, and government partners. It will serve as an educational hub, where people can learn about gorillas, and scientists can learn more about how to keep gorillas protected.

Portia and I had the opportunity to visit the site where the campus will be built, as well as the Fossey Fund's current headquarters. I actually got to sit at Dian's desk—the exact same one where she worked in her tent in the forest over 50 years ago. I saw the notebooks she used to keep track of her observations and even her original typewriter. If you don't know what that is, google "old-timey laptop."

Portia and I also got to climb the mountain to go see the mountain gorillas. (Now I get why they're called mountain gorillas!) That journey was one of the most beautiful, emotional, breath-taking, and mud-filled journeys I've ever been on. It was incredible.

You may not know this, but humans share 98 percent of their DNA with gorillas. Gorillas are extraordinary animals. They're brilliant and compassionate, and it's because of Dian Fossey that we know as much about them as we do. Since Dian began her conservation efforts in Rwanda, the mountain gorilla population has more than doubled. It's so important that they are given the chance to thrive in their natural habitats, and I can't wait to see what the future holds.

When I was a kid staring at that poster on my bedroom wall, I never dreamed that I would actually get to experience the gorillas like Dian Fossey did. I never could have imagined being so close to her work, and I am so proud to be part of it now.

I'm excited for you to learn more about Dian Fossey and everything she accomplished as you read this book. She is my hero, and I hope you too will want to help carry on her extraordinary legacy of protecting mountain gorillas.

Holding Hands

Slowly, scientist Dian Fossey moved closer to a young male mountain gorilla she had named Peanuts. As if showing off, Peanuts beat his chest, threw leaves in the air, slapped the foliage around him, and strutted. Then, watching for her reaction, he moved closer to Dian's side.

Dian scratched her scalp; then Peanuts began to scratch.

She lay back in the foliage and extended her hand.

He moved closer—touching his fingers to hers.

As far as Dian knew, a wild gorilla had never before held hands with a human being.

Peanuts gave a whirling chest beat and moved away to join his gorilla friends.

Dian Fossey wept tears of joy.

Dian and Peanuts reach their hands out to each other.

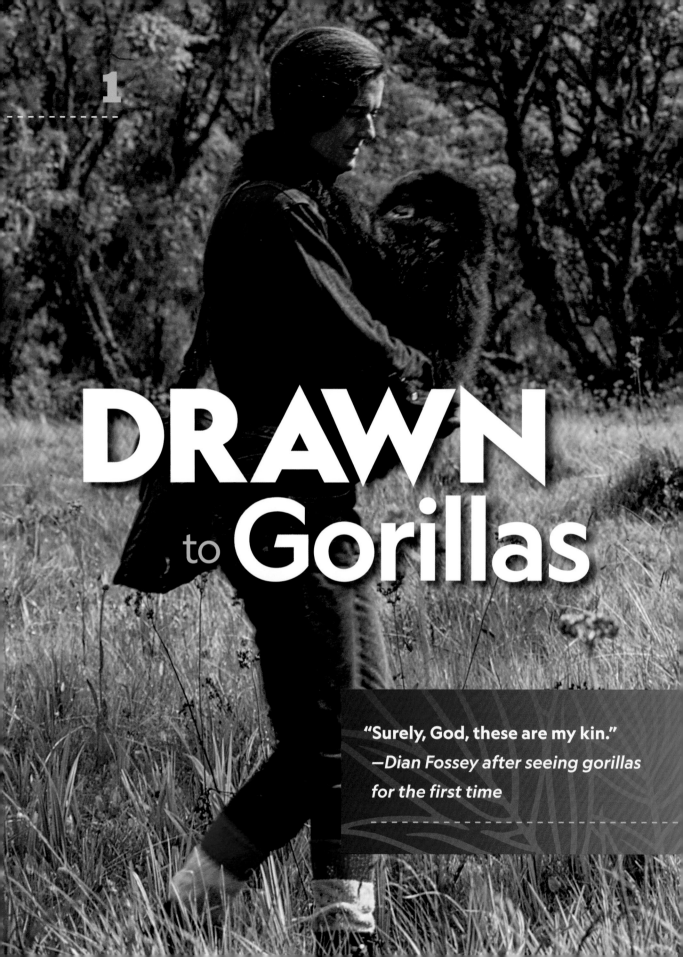

DRAWN to Gorillas

"Surely, God, these are my kin."
—Dian Fossey after seeing gorillas
for the first time

I

n 1944, when Dian Fossey was 12 years old, she developed an elaborate scheme. She had heard about European children suffering from the destruction of World War II and decided that she must somehow get to Europe and help them. From her home in San Francisco, California, U.S.A., she managed to reach the city docks where she could board a ship. But that was as far as she got.

In Rwanda, Dian Fossey takes a walk with young mountain gorillas Coco and Pucker.

11

Dian as a young girl

Dian didn't manage to aid the children of Europe, but the next rescue mission she undertook would be more successful. She would travel halfway around the world to devote herself to mountain gorillas, a species so scarce they faced extinction. Her decades of work studying the gorillas made all the difference to these incredible great apes.

Born in San Francisco on January 16, 1932, Dian grew up during the Great Depression, a time when the majority of Americans lacked money or resources to keep food on the table. Times were tough, as was her family life: Dian's father, George Fossey, suffered from alcoholism. After Dian's mother, Kitty, divorced George, the young girl longed to spend more time with him. She wanted to have a relationship with her absent father, yet even the mention of his name in the house was discouraged. As a result, Dian did not see him again for years.

Kitty eventually remarried, and her new husband, Richard Price, made a lot of money as a businessman. He was a stern man who never developed a supportive

During the Great Depression of the 1930s, people across the United States lost their jobs. In cities such as Los Angeles (left), unemployed people lined up to receive soup and bread to eat.

San Francisco in the 1930s

Like cities all across the United States, San Francisco, Dian Fossey's hometown, faced economic struggles during the Great Depression. Businesses closed and many people lost their jobs. But even in hard times, the California city was bustling with life. People packed into cable cars that traversed the city's steep hills, riding to the market for groceries or to Fleishhacker Pool, the United States' largest public pool at the time, for an afternoon swim. Building of the iconic Golden Gate Bridge started in 1933, bringing new jobs to the city. Four years later, the bridge officially opened. In 1939, the city held the Golden Gate International Exposition, drawing people from all over the world to celebrate the city's growth.

- -

In 1939 and 1940, people flocked to the Golden Gate International Exposition, located on the newly made Treasure Island *(top)*. On San Francisco's mainland, cable cars transported people across the city *(bottom)*.

The Misunderstood Gorilla

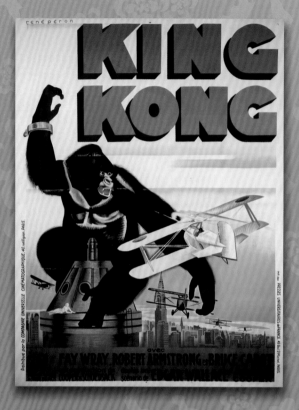

rior to Dian's pioneering study, most Americans connected the word "gorilla" with the image of the terrifying monster King Kong. Often depicted baring his teeth, Kong beat his chest standing atop the Empire State Building and plucked airplanes out of midair. Many people thought of gorillas only as ferocious and dangerous. But biologist George Schaller challenged these widely held beliefs. His two books, *The Mountain Gorilla* and *The Year of the Gorilla*, chronicled his study of mountain gorillas in the Virunga volcanoes of central Africa. Schaller boldly stated that all the material that had appeared about gorillas was "sensational, irresponsible, and exaggerated ... with little concern for the truth." Building on Schaller's eye-opening work, Dian would extend understanding of the personalities of these peaceful, plant-eating animals and educate the public about the real nature of one of humans' closest relatives.

A giant gorilla towers over New York City in this poster for the 1933 film *King Kong*.

relationship with Dian. He insisted that she eat most of her meals in the kitchen with the family housekeeper. That turned out to be only one way Dian felt isolated from and rejected by her parents. Even as an adult, Dian loathed her stepfather; she would spit on the ground at the mention of his name.

Dian's dealings with her mother were also a struggle. Kitty, a professional model, disapproved of her daughter's appearance. By her late teens, Dian had grown to be six feet tall, and she felt gangly and awkward. Knowing she did not measure up to her mother's standards, she remained insecure about how she looked all her life.

Lacking support or much affection from her parents, Dian found love through her relationships with animals. Though she desperately wanted a pet—any pet—her parents would not allow it. They finally permitted a goldfish, which quickly died. Dian cried for days.

ALTHOUGH DIAN'S PARENTS DIDN'T WANT AN ANIMAL IN THE HOUSE, they did approve of horse-riding lessons and provided them for their daughter. Dian loved spending time with horses. In high school, she joined the riding team and excelled as one of its best members. One magical summer, a ranch in Montana hired Dian to care for horses. She enjoyed spending the entire day with the animals so much that it did not even seem like a job.

After she completed high school, Dian attended a business school but was not interested in the classes. She then enrolled in the pre-veterinary medical course at the University of California, Davis. It seemed an ideal path, because it would mean sharing her life with animals. Working weekends, holidays, and summers

Dian graduated in 1954 from San José State University. Tower Hall (*below*) is the oldest building on the campus.

to pay for her schooling, Dian did well in plant and animal studies. But she dropped out during her second year because she could not master physics and chemistry. Instead, she enrolled in San José State University for a degree in occupational therapy. This training would make it possible for Dian to help children with physical and intellectual disabilities.

AFTER GRADUATING, DIAN COULDN'T WAIT to leave California—she wanted a place where she could flourish on her own. A children's hospital in Louisville, Kentucky, hired her to be an occupational therapy director, and so the city became Dian's first destination. Many of the children developed polio and needed, as Dian said, "a tremendous amount of care and kindness." In addition to her assigned duties as a therapist, she painted a *Wizard of Oz* mural on a wall to brighten the space and enticed squirrels to come out of the woods to amuse the children.

In Louisville, she made lifelong friends, something she'd go on to do wherever she traveled. Like her mother, Dian had a flair for fashion and enjoyed wearing gold jewelry and beautiful expensive clothes. She relished being the center of attention and entranced any crowd with her storytelling. With a "marvelous sense of humor" and a quick smile, she amused people by telling jokes. Over fancy dinners and at parties, Dian delighted in entertaining and pampering her friends. A forceful personality, full of emotion, she seemed larger than life.

Dian not only surrounded herself with friends, but animals, too. In Louisville, she lived outside of town, in a rundown cottage on an old farm, and spent her free time with

Dian meets with children on her 1963 trip to Africa.

Mary and Louis Leakey

Born to British missionary parents, Louis Leakey grew up in Kenya, Africa. He received his doctorate from the University of Cambridge, in England, after studying anthropology, archaeology, and African prehistory. In 1934, he wrote a book about human origins called *Adam's Ancestors,* and Mary Douglas Nicol, an artist who specialized in paleoanthropology, illustrated it.

Louis and Mary wed in 1937 and moved to Africa, hoping to prove Charles Darwin's theory that human life originated there. In 1948, while excavating Olduvai Gorge in Tanzania, East Africa, Mary found a fossilized skull of an ancestor of apes and humans called *Proconsul africanus.* Estimated to be about 18 million years old, the skull proved human origins were much older than the scientific community believed at the time. During their lives, Mary and Louis discovered many more remains of the earliest humans and set up a foundation to pursue the study of human origins.

Anthropologists Mary and Louis Leakey, holding a bone fragment of an early human, pose for a photograph.

the resident raccoons, possums, cattle, scores of dogs, and barn cats. But she longed to see other kinds of creatures. After talking to an acquaintance who had been on an African safari, Dian planned one for herself, thrilled by the possibility of all the species she would be able to see on one trip.

She drew on all of her savings and obtained a loan. In 1963, Dian hired a personal guide for seven glorious weeks to take her through several countries—Kenya, Tanzania, Uganda, the Democratic Republic of the Congo (DRC), and Southern Rhodesia (now Zimbabwe). In Tanzania's Serengeti National Park she saw thousands of animals, including elephants, rhinos, flocks of flamingos, zebras, lions, and leopards.

Her travel guide had also arranged for her to see the excavation sites of famous paleoanthropologists Louis and Mary Leakey, who in Tanzania's Olduvai Gorge had unearthed remains of an early ancestor of modern humans, *Homo habilis.* Several different accounts exist about what happened that day. Dian may or may not have actually gotten a chance to speak to Louis Leakey. But the site made a great impression on her—while there she slipped, twisted her ankle, and almost threw up.

Though she struggled to walk, Dian traveled on to her next destination—the mountainous terrain in the DRC—in search of mountain gorillas. After she and her guide had made a difficult climb, made worse by Dian's injury, they arrived in the area of a mountain gorilla family. At first Dian heard a series of high-pitched, terrifying screams. Then she saw "in a dappled half-light of a forest clearing, a group of six adult mountain gorillas." The animals returned Dian's gaze, and she was able to see that they were "beautiful creatures with thick, velvety fur, shiny black faces and warm brown eyes." They beat their chests, broke off branches, scratched themselves, and yawned. The group looked like they were having a picnic, enjoying the air and sunshine. Dian Fossey felt an immediate connection with these animals—she fell completely in love.

Nestled among dense vegetation in the mountains of Rwanda, a group of mountain gorillas rest together.

DIAN RETURNED TO HER work in Louisville a changed human being. She could think of nothing but those animals, and now she had a goal: to return to Africa to spend time with gorillas. She began using photographs of her trip to write articles about mountain gorillas for the local newspaper. And then a small miracle happened. In the spring of 1966, Louis Leakey came to Louisville, Kentucky, as part of a lecture tour.

This aerial photograph shows Louisville, Kentucky, in the 1950s. Dian moved to Louisville in 1955 and lived there for nearly 11 years, working as an occupational therapist.

At the end of his inspiring talk, in which he spoke about Jane Goodall and her work with chimpanzees, Dian waited in line to meet him. As soon as she stood before him, she pressed her newspaper articles into Leakey's hands. Looking over them, he asked her some questions and requested that she meet him early the next day. Leakey had always preferred field researchers with minds uncluttered by scientific theory. Dian was just the kind of amateur he sought out—enthusiastic, ambitious, and gutsy.

That next morning Leakey had some important things to tell her. Coincidentally, he had been hunting for someone to undertake a long-term field assignment observing gorillas. In his work on the origins of humans, Leakey felt that great apes should be studied in the wild to learn more about how the first humans behaved. Given Dian's interest, he believed she could conduct such a study. Dian worried that, at 34, she might be too old to begin field research. But Leakey, relying as he always did on his instincts, thought neither her lack of scientific training nor her age would be impediments. He simply needed to raise the appropriate funds for such a mission.

While Leakey worked to find funding, Dian changed her life. She quit her job, learned Swahili, and took a course in primatology, the study of monkeys and apes. She spent much of her time "virtually memorizing" two books written by biologist

George Schaller, *The Mountain Gorilla* and *The Year of the Gorilla*. Leakey wanted her to expand on Schaller's research with a longer-term study that would reveal more about gorilla life and families.

AFTER MANY MONTHS, Leakey made good on his promise to find funding. In December 1966, Dian flew to Washington, D.C., to meet the staff of the National Geographic Society, which provided money for her to research mountain gorillas.

Clouds loom over the Virunga Mountains, which stretch along the border of the Democratic Republic of the Congo, Rwanda, and Uganda.

Zoologist George Schaller *(opposite)* has studied many animals, including mountain gorillas, lions, giant pandas, and wild sheep.

Although Louis Leakey had great faith in Dian, others who met her formed a different opinion. Dian was suffering from pneumonia during the Washington, D.C., visit and so she did not exactly appear to be a researcher in the peak of physical health. At least one official at National Geographic wrote to Leakey, questioning her fitness for the position.

Actually, the odds of Dian's failing were quite high. Without training, she would be thrown into situations she had never encountered. She would need to survive long periods of time in the wilderness, far away from doctors and hospitals, as she dealt with broken bones, headaches, fevers, and a variety of serious illnesses. She would also be a foreigner in an area of the world that was on the brink of civil unrest. And she would be living in a culture that was not her own, with its own language, customs, and rules.

At this point in her life, Dian Fossey had accomplished nothing that would suggest she could become one of the most important animal researchers of the 20th century. A determined fighter, Dian did not run from adversity. She now had a mentor in Louis Leakey, who believed she could be his gorilla researcher. And she was motivated to return to these animals and show the world that this was a species worth saving. As she set out to the remote Virunga Mountains, Dian would rely not on her credentials but on her inner strength to become the scientist few believed she could be.

THE TRIMATES

During the 1960s and 1970s, Louis Leakey recruited three different women who were all interested in studying animals: Jane Goodall, Biruté Mary Galdikas, and Dian Fossey. He encouraged each of them to study a different primate in their natural habitat, something he believed would be a key to understanding human evolution. He called the women "the Trimates" and helped them raise money for their research. Though each followed a unique path, all made major contributions to our understanding of the great apes and successfully completed more hours of field research on them than any other scientist at the time.

JANE GOODALL

As a child, Jane Goodall never met an animal that she didn't find fascinating; she observed earthworms, chickens, dogs, and birds, trying to figure out why they behaved as they did. With Louis Leakey's help, Jane traveled to Tanganyika (now Tanzania) in 1960, and set up a research station in what is now Gombe Stream National Park. Not only did she become the world's foremost chimpanzee expert, but she has been a tireless advocate for animal rights and conservation, traveling and speaking all over the world on behalf of all creatures great and small.

BIRUTÉ MARY GALDIKAS

In 1971, Biruté Mary Galdikas traveled to a remote location in Borneo to set up Camp Leakey to study orangutans. Because of the challenging terrain and the fact that orangutans frequently travel high above the ground through the rainforest canopy, scientists knew little about these elusive animals. But unlike other researchers, Biruté never left her research station and has managed it as one of the longest continuing studies of any wild mammal under a single scientist. Today, her Orangutan Care Center and Quarantine has rehabilitated and released more than 500 orangutans back into the wild.

Biruté Galdikas (*right*) rescues and raises orphaned orangutans at her camp inside Tanjung Puting National Park on the Indonesian island of Borneo.

When Jane Goodall (*left*) observed chimpanzees using tools, she wrote to Louis Leakey: "Now we must redefine 'tool,' redefine 'man,' or accept chimpanzees as humans."

A MISSION
in the Mountains

"Neither destiny nor fate took me to Africa. Nor was it romance. I had a deep wish to see and live with wild animals in a world that hadn't yet been completely changed by humans." —*Dian Fossey*

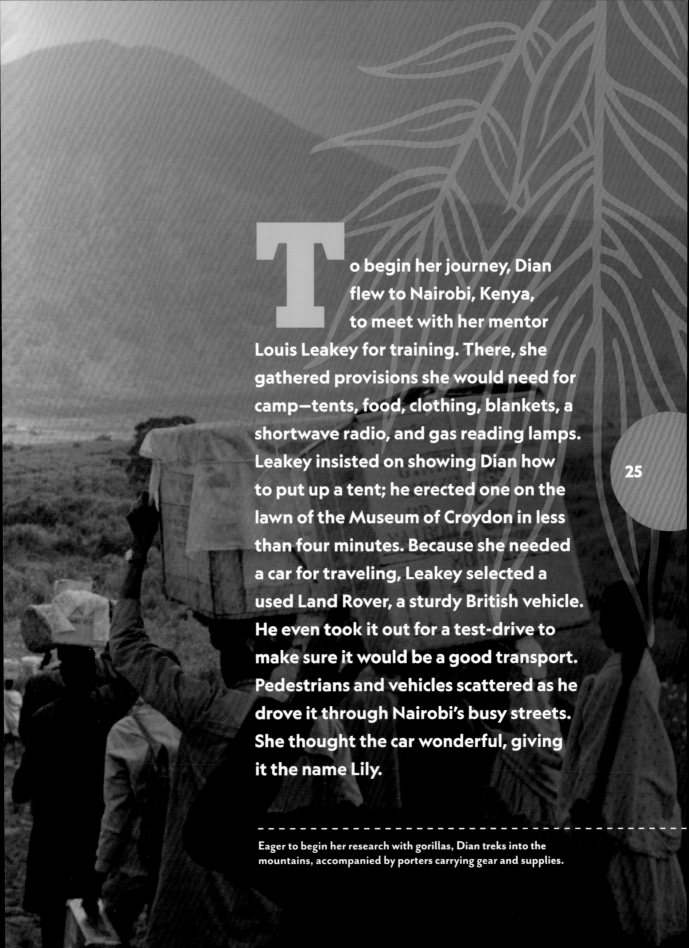

To begin her journey, Dian flew to Nairobi, Kenya, to meet with her mentor Louis Leakey for training. There, she gathered provisions she would need for camp—tents, food, clothing, blankets, a shortwave radio, and gas reading lamps. Leakey insisted on showing Dian how to put up a tent; he erected one on the lawn of the Museum of Croydon in less than four minutes. Because she needed a car for traveling, Leakey selected a used Land Rover, a sturdy British vehicle. He even took it out for a test-drive to make sure it would be a good transport. Pedestrians and vehicles scattered as he drove it through Nairobi's busy streets. She thought the car wonderful, giving it the name Lily.

Eager to begin her research with gorillas, Dian treks into the mountains, accompanied by porters carrying gear and supplies.

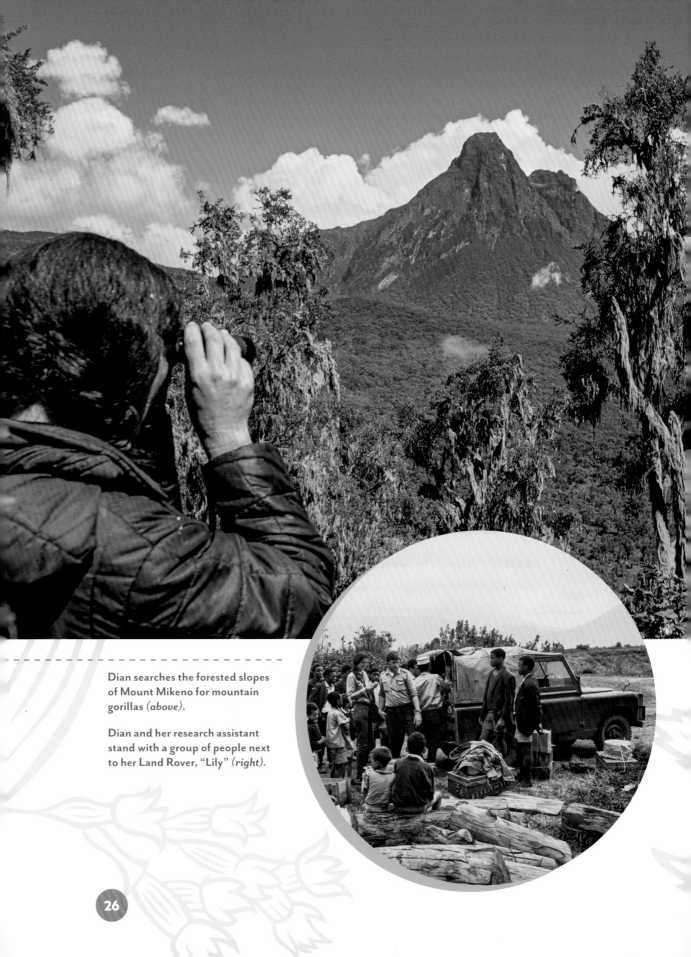

Dian searches the forested slopes of Mount Mikeno for mountain gorillas (*above*).

Dian and her research assistant stand with a group of people next to her Land Rover, "Lily" (*right*).

AFTER DIAN DEPARTED NAIROBI, SHE TRAVELED TO
Tanzania. The 1966 Christmas holiday was approaching and
Leakey had arranged for Dian to spend it with Jane Goodall and
her husband, Hugo van Lawick. Through her research, Jane had
discovered that chimps could contract polio, and she was waiting
on a shipment of a vaccine to help the animals. Once the medicine
arrived, Dian traveled with Jane to Gombe Stream Game Reserve.
For two days, Jane showed the new recruit how to collect and
record information and how to establish a successful camp.

Now Dian was eager to set up her own camp. She had chosen
the Virunga Mountains of the Democratic Republic of the Congo,
the site where George Schaller had conducted his studies and she
had first seen mountain gorillas. Excited about setting out on her
next chapter, Dian arrived in the DRC and found that her on-the-
ground guides, Alan and Joan Root, had serious reservations
about her plan. The DRC's military had become unpredictable in
terms of its support of foreigners living in their country. At any
moment, they all might be asked to leave.

Dian rejected their pleas to revise her plans and instead hired
two armed guards and a few dozen Congolese porters, and began
a slow and painful 4,000-foot (1,220-m) trek up Mount Mikeno—
named "the naked one" because of its bald summit. The rainforest
that covered the mountain made the air cold, wet, and foggy.
Ascending the steep muddy slopes, Dian, with lungs scarred by
years of smoking, struggled to breathe in the damp air as she went
higher and higher in the mountain. Her limbs felt heavy; it was
often painful to put one foot in front of the other. She would take
a few steps and then have to stop. Another few steps and stop
again. Some of the sights encouraged her—the beautiful *Hagenia*
trees that lined the path and the roaming wild buffalo. But the trek
remained difficult every step of the way. Finally, the party arrived
in the Kabara meadow, a breathtaking and pristine place. Dian
considered it one of the loveliest places on Earth.

For two days Alan Root helped Dian set up her camp—a latrine with burlap curtains around it for privacy, a cabin for the porters, and rain barrels to capture freshwater. Dian would live in a 7-by-10-foot (2-by-3-m) tent; it housed her papers and the typewriter she used every night to record observations. Alan gave Dian a crash course in tracking—how to follow gorilla footprints, to observe the broken branches that indicated movement, and to find spoor (gorilla dung). Over the years Dian would grow appreciative of how much could be learned from gorilla dung.

THEN ON JANUARY 15, 1967, THE DAY BEFORE DIAN'S 35TH BIRTHDAY, Alan wished her luck and headed back down the mountain. Dian panicked as she watched him depart: "He was my last link with civilization as I had always known it … I clung on to my tent pole simply to avoid running after him."

Feeling lonely and strange in her new location, Dian refused even to listen to the shortwave radio that Leakey had insisted she bring, believing it would make her feel even more isolated. But soon Sanwekwe, a Congolese

Dian relied heavily on her Congolese guide, Sanwekwe (*below left*), to track gorillas through the mountains.

A family of mountain gorillas—
called a troop—relaxes together
and looks for food.

park guard and experienced gorilla tracker, arrived in camp and started taking her out on the trails.

Four days after Dian's arrival in the DRC, she and Sanwekwe located an adult gorilla sunning on a horizontal tree trunk. Then they came upon a young male who at first watched them, then hooted and beat his chest until several other members of his family appeared. Clearly this gorilla family, which Dian named Group 1, had already adapted to the presence of humans. Dian sat with them for three hours. It took Jane Goodall and Biruté Galdikas months before they could get close enough to chimps and orangutans to actually observe them for any period of time.

Gorilla sightings made some of the problems Dian faced bearable. Her living conditions would have challenged any but the most determined. In this area of the Virunga volcanoes, rain fell for almost two hours every day. Every surface felt cold, dark, and often muddy. Even on sunny days, the slippery and tangled paths made hiking difficult. Most of Dian's walking had to take place at a 45-degree angle, which meant a steep uphill climb. Stinging nettles felt like electric needles as they pierced her skin. Fierce safari ants bit through two layers of her clothing.

Every night she went back to her dark and wet tent, sat hunched over her typewriter, and recorded her daily observations. Living simply, she obtained few possessions in her

Animals of the Virungas

The Virunga Mountains teem with biodiversity. Species big and small can be spotted hopping, grazing, and flying across the landscape. Here are a few of the animals that live in this wondrous place.

Mammals

Golden monkey

African buffalo

Side-striped jackal

Amphibians

Karisimbi forest tree frog

Brown reed frog

Friedrich's squeaker frog

Birds

Rwenzori batis

Rwenzori double-collared sunbird

Rwenzori turaco

first months. In time, she acquired her first pets: a chicken, Lucy, and a rooster, Dezi. They not only kept her company, but Lucy also laid fresh eggs. With almost nothing to distract her, Dian made amazing strides in her research.

Slowly, and with Sanwekwe's help, Dian learned how to become a better tracker. She tried to remain invisible to the gorillas so as not to startle them. The first thing she noticed was their smell, a "musky-barnyard, humanlike scent." Then she heard them, often the *pok-pok* sound of chest beats. Finally, she caught sight of them.

But Dian knew she couldn't remain invisible. She needed the gorillas to accept her so she could stay close to them for more than a few minutes. So Dian would

This drawing, sketched by a researcher, shows the unique pattern of wrinkles above this gorilla's nose.

mimic their behavior. At first her efforts were modest: She'd walk on her knuckles, chomp on plant stems just as they did, scratch herself, and make gorilla noises. But some of these efforts proved counterproductive. She had often slapped her hands against her thighs to re-create the sound of their chest-beating until she realized this noise alarmed the gorillas. Dian definitely got their attention, but she caused them to flee.

In time, she learned how to identify individual gorillas—by their noses. Just as no two humans have the same fingerprints, no two gorillas have the same nose print (the shape and space around their nostrils). So as Dian watched the gorillas with binoculars, she sketched their noses so she could remember them when she saw them again. She later photographed individual gorillas to get more specific images. Once she was able to identify the subtle variations of gorilla noses, Dian could tell the animals apart, give them names, and begin to understand their individual and family histories.

Though she lived frugally and ate sparsely, Dian had settled into a somewhat comfortable routine after six months of research. She could only get food when she traveled to the nearest town, a two-hour drive from the base of the mountain. There, she stocked up once a month on "cans of hot dogs, Spam, powdered milk, margarine, corned beef, tuna ... noodles, spaghetti, oatmeal, and bags of sweets." When these ran out, she resorted to potatoes in every form. Fortunately, she really liked potatoes.

EVEN WITH THE RUSTIC LIVING QUARTERS and inadequate diet, Dian would have stayed at her camp for years. But just as Alan and Joan Root had feared, in July 1967, the Democratic Republic of the Congo's government alerted her that she was no longer welcome. A state of emergency had been declared, and foreigners were ordered out of the country. Dian had no choice but to pack up camp and head out. She was heartbroken to leave and spent most of the trip down the mountain in tears: "I never fully realized what the place meant to me until I had to give it up."

As she was trying to get out of the country, Dian was taken captive by the military. She told many different versions of this story over the years. In some she outwitted her captors and made a dramatic escape; in others she had been held as a prisoner in a cage. Whatever happened, she feared for her safety; the military police had been arresting and sometimes killing foreigners. Once safe, Dian wrote to her parents, "everything is fairly jumbled up now." She had no camp and no base to continue her work. She also had no intention of giving up on the gorillas. She headed to Nairobi to see Louis Leakey again. At first he offered to help her research different animals—lowland gorillas or orangutans. But Dian felt completely devoted to mountain gorillas. Instead, she begged for funds to set up a camp in the Rwandan mountains;

To gain the gorillas' trust, Dian mimicked their behavior. Here she munches on wild celery, one of their favorite foods.

Gorilla Species

All gorilla life centers around families, which can vary from 2 to 50 members, depending on how many females and children exist. The leader, a strong silverback male gorilla (named because of the stripe of silver hairs that covers the backs of males like a saddle when they mature), protects his family and helps them move to safe locations to find enough food. There are two species of gorillas, each with two subspecies:

Eastern Gorillas (*Gorilla beringei*)

❯ **Grauer's gorillas,** formerly known as eastern lowland gorillas, live only in the DRC. They cover the widest altitudinal range of the gorillas, living in forests ranging from 1,968 to 9,514 feet (600 to 2,900 m).

❮ **Mountain gorillas** make their homes in high-altitude rainforests. Their long, thick fur helps them survive the colder temperatures in these locations.

Western Gorillas (*Gorilla gorilla*)

❯ **Western lowland gorillas** have redder and grayer fur than the other species. They can be found in Cameroon, the Central African Republic, Angola, the DRC, Nigeria, Equatorial Guinea, and Gabon.

❮ **Cross River gorillas** are the world's rarest gorilla species. Found in an area along the Nigeria–Cameroon border, these elusive apes have been the most difficult for scientists to study.

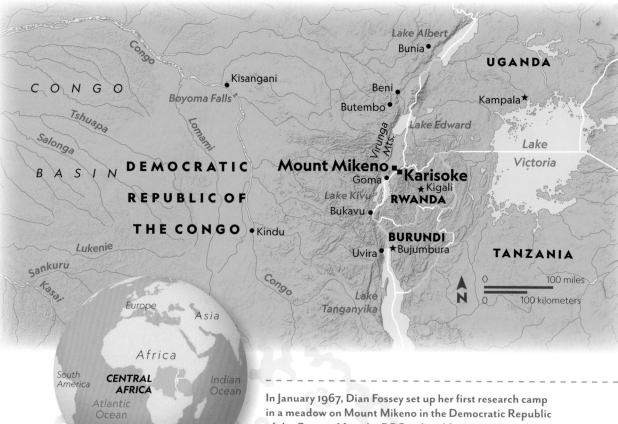

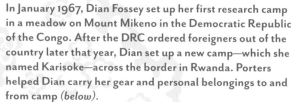

In January 1967, Dian Fossey set up her first research camp in a meadow on Mount Mikeno in the Democratic Republic of the Congo. After the DRC ordered foreigners out of the country later that year, Dian set up a new camp—which she named Karisoke—across the border in Rwanda. Porters helped Dian carry her gear and personal belongings to and from camp (*below*).

after all, gorillas paid no attention to the boundaries of countries. Many of the families she had studied regularly traveled this terrain to forage for food.

Convinced by her determination, Leakey raised money once again from National Geographic and the Wilkie Brothers Foundation. He faced severe criticism from those in Nairobi who knew of the recent events. Dian would still be in danger so close to the border of the DRC. But as Leakey said to her: "If people like you and me and Jane ... put our personal safety first ... we would never get any work done at all."

With Leakey's continued support, Dian hired a new team of porters and began the long climb into Rwanda's Volcanoes National Park, a protected area between two extinct volcanoes, Mount Karisimbi and Mount Bisoke. Although she wanted to pitch her tent quickly and get started, she trusted her local guides to advise her on an ideal spot. After a long trek, they led her to a meadow on a 10,000-foot (3,000-m)-high plateau.

At 4:30 p.m. on September 24, 1967, Dian established a modest two-tent camp-site, which she named Karisoke. A few minutes after they began setting it up, Dian heard an unmistakable noise.

Pok-pok. The sound of gorillas beating their chests echoed through gathering darkness.

This site, which would become the Karisoke Research Center, would serve as Dian's home for the next 18 years.

VIRUNGA LANDSCAPES

With landscapes ranging from humid swamps to lakes of lava to snowcapped peaks, the region in East Africa known as the Virunga Massif is one of the most biologically diverse places on Earth. The area contains the Virunga Mountains, a chain of eight volcanoes that stretch along the border of Rwanda, the Democratic Republic of the Congo (DRC), and Uganda. It covers three national parks: the DRC's Virunga National Park, Uganda's Mgahinga Gorilla National Park, and Rwanda's Volcanoes National Park, where Dian Fossey established the Karisoke Research Center between two of Virunga's volcanic mountains: Bisoke and Karisimbi.

SAVANNAS

Situated in the center of the DRC's Virunga National Park, the Rwindi Plains and Ishasha Valley are home to a variety of wildlife. Lions prowl the Ishasha Valley. On the Rwindi Plains, buffalo roam in herds of 50 to 500 individuals. Elephants, hippos, antelope, warthogs, and hyenas are found here, too.

African elephants gather in herds across the grassy plains of Virunga National Park.

GLACIERS

At the eastern edge of the Virunga Massif lie the Rwenzori Mountains. The tallest peaks in the Rwenzori range are covered in snow year-round. In the early 1900s, there were 43 glaciers scattered across these mountains. Today, less than half of those remain. Scientists believe climate change has caused the glaciers to recede.

Glaciers, waterfalls, and lakes are found in Rwenzori Mountains National Park, in Uganda.

VOLCANOES

The oldest of the eight volcanoes in the Virunga Mountains is called Mount Sabyinyo. Known as "Old Man's Teeth" for its peaks that look like jagged teeth, Mount Sabyinyo dates back to the Pleistocene era, a time period that began about 2.6 million years ago. The two most active volcanoes in Africa are found in the Virungas: Nyamuragira and Nyiragongo. Deep inside the crater of Mount Nyiragongo lies the world's largest bubbling lava lake.

Mount Bisoke, a dormant volcano in the Virunga Mountains, stands roughly 12,100 feet (3,700 m) tall. A lake sits atop its flat peak.

WETLANDS

The Semliki, Rwindi, and Rutshuru Rivers run through the Virunga Mountains, all connecting into Lake Edward at the heart of the DRC's Virunga National Park. Along the riverbanks, hippos take a dip in the shallow water. Thanks to conservation efforts, Virunga National Park is now home to Africa's largest concentration of the species—roughly 2,500 hippopotamuses live inside the park.

The Rutshuru River is a popular spot for hippos and other wildlife to visit.

BEFRIENDING
the Greatest of the Great Apes

Grateful to be in a new site, Dian quickly established her routine of searching for and observing gorillas during the day and typing up her notes at night. But she also made plans for more permanent buildings in Karisoke. After a few months, she worked with her staff to build a spacious 12-by-20-foot (4-by-6-m) cabin.

Dian shows her field notebook to orphaned mountain gorillas Coco and Pucker.

"The more you learn about the dignity of the gorilla, the more you want to avoid people." —Dian Fossey

This new home provided some comforts for Dian: She painted the walls green, hung bright yellow cotton curtains, and decorated with wall hangings, floor mats, masks, and other local items. Two wood-burning stoves gave both heat and light in the evening. Now her evening quarters seemed more inviting.

Her windows looked out onto *Hagenia* trees covered with moss, lichens, and orchids, a sight she found stunning: "They look like they are floating, in all the shades of the green rainforest." At night she heard the sounds of wildlife all around her. Buffalo came to drink at a nearby creek. Elephants trumpeted and bellowed. Tree hyraxes screeched.

LEAVING THIS COZY CABIN EACH MORNING, Dian climbed to the area of one of her gorilla families, bringing along a camera, a notebook, and binoculars. She hid behind vegetation so as not to scare them and slowly accustomed them to her presence. Unlike the gorillas in the DRC, who had mostly adapted to humans who came as tourists, the

gorillas in this area had only seen humans who might harm them. It took Dian longer to win their trust.

Each day, after she sat hidden for a while, she'd begin to mimic gorilla behavior:

She groomed herself.

She crawled along the trails rather than walking, so as not to startle them.

She pretended to chew on gorilla delicacies like bamboo; she crunched her jaws so it would sound like she was consuming nettles.

With her tape recorder, Dian captured dozens of the vocalizations that gorillas made. She also learned to interpret and mimic gorilla communication.

Naoom, naoom, naoom meant food is served.

Hum, hum, a soft purring, was a happy sound.

A hoot expressed curiosity or an alert.

Piglike grunts settled disputes.

As vegetable-eaters, gorillas produced a lot of low-rumbling belches, *ummwaah.* Dian named this sound the "belch vocalization," or BV.

Gradually, she mastered how to speak and act like a gorilla.

After countless hours with these gorillas, Dian began to understand their behaviors. Gorillas loved to play with one another and everything around them. The younger apes swung through the trees as if they lived in one large, mossy gymnasium; like human babies, they enjoyed examining and touching their toes. After they grew comfortable with Dian, the gorillas would seize any object she carried—and even tried to take her boot off her foot. Sometimes one of the gorillas snatched her gloves or her notebook. To her horror, they would then eat the pages.

Dian marveled at how gentle the huge silverback males could be with their offspring. They would pick up, examine, and groom the young gorillas. Then they played with the youngsters, allowing them to jump up and down on their huge stomachs.

All the gorillas seemed to adore basking in the sun and being close to one another. Sometimes, if she was lucky, Dian would hear them singing, usually in the sunshine while eating. Their songs sounded like a mixture of a dog whining and someone humming in the bath. When she heard them, she tried blending in her own voice.

ALL THESE OBSERVATIONS HELPED DIAN UNDERSTAND THAT these huge creatures were shy, gentle giants—peaceful plant-eaters. Only when the gorilla family was threatened would the reigning silverback male rise to protect them. During 2,000 hours of gorilla observation, Dian rarely encountered what might be called aggressive behavior.

Other Animal Friends

While at Karisoke, Dian provided a home for all kinds of creatures, including her much beloved dog, Cindy. Dian's other various pets included a mischievous and very destructive blue monkey named Kima. Kima would roam around camp, scream at visitors, and often bite them. She liked to bite the heads off Dian's matches and had particular tastes—she enjoyed french fries, but only their creamy insides. During her time at Karisoke, Dian's pet menagerie increased and constantly changed: There were Charles and Yvonne (ravens), Dot and Dash (gray parrots), and even a family of rats. Even buffalo and antelope wandered into the camp and played with the domesticated animals.

- -

Among the animals that Dian cared for at Karisoke was a blue monkey named Kima.

The popular images of large, angry gorillas—like King Kong on the Empire State Building—were simply false.

A silverback male pauses in a clearing with his family. When traveling, silverback leaders walk first to protect their group.

Even so, Dian had to learn to avoid dangerous situations. If the group included a newborn baby, the adults could be quite fierce. When an angry silverback gorilla protects his family, he makes an "explosive, half-screaming sound" that shatters the stillness. The first time Dian heard this noise was the first time she felt afraid of gorillas. That day, a group of males, screaming loudly, charged her, so she sank to the ground in a submissive posture; one of the males recognized her and stopped the charge. They continued to scream at her but finally went away. That day was not the only time she'd faced difficulties in the field. Gorilla observation required a great deal of patience—and it tested Dian's bravery.

After Dian had made some progress getting the gorillas to trust her, *National Geographic* magazine sent photographer and filmmaker Robert Campbell to document Dian's headway. He captured a groundbreaking moment between Dian and a young male gorilla called Peanuts. As Campbell filmed, Peanuts beat his chest, then came to Dian's side and slowly reached out his hand, touching his fingers to hers. After that interaction, Dian cabled Louis Leakey. "I'VE FINALLY BEEN ACCEPTED BY A GORILLA." Leakey carried that cable in his pocket for several years and would pull it out and read it at lectures.

Dian leans toward Digit and shows him an object. Dian gave Digit his name after seeing that one of his fingers was injured, probably by a poacher's trap.

As she encountered different groups of gorillas, Dian enjoyed discovering their individual personalities. She first met one of her favorites, Puck, when the ape was a youngster. At first Dian believed Puck was male, but the young ape was actually a female. Puck constantly wanted to examine the contents of Dian's backpack. She looked at the camera, its lenses, and the binoculars. Puck would take the binoculars and use them to survey the landscape like an explorer. But she also pointed them on the ground and examined the foliage. She would wiggle her fingers in front of the lenses and then remove them to look at her fingers. All these activities made Dian believe that Puck used binoculars as humans would. Offered a *National Geographic* magazine, Puck flicked through the pages, showing particular interest in large color photographs of faces.

Dian met another favorite, Digit, when he was young, about five years old. Spotting Dian, he would roll over on his back and kick his legs in the air. "He often invited play by flopping over on to his back," Dian recalled, "as if to say 'How can you resist me?'" He frequently touched her hair and clothing. He hugged Dian, and they wrestled with each other and played together. Once Dian observed Digit tumble into the lap of a mature gorilla, Uncle Bert. Bert picked a handful of flowers and brushed them back and forth on Digit's face to tickle the youngster. Digit laughed and gave "a big toothy grin."

Digit also loved to examine Dian's objects. Once Dian brought a candy bar for a snack and playfully dropped it in a tree stump. Then she asked Digit to get it for her. He obeyed as if he understood, using his long arm to pull it out. But evidently, the smell was not to his taste: After examining the candy bar, he threw it back where he had found it.

BUT AS DIAN GOT CLOSER TO THE GORILLAS, SHE DISCOVERED that her scientific detachment vanished. They had become more than just subjects to study; they were now friends and companions. She began to worry about their health and well-being. That concern led Dian to focus on the people and practices that threatened "her gorillas," as she called them. Volcanoes National Park measured only 62 square miles (161 sq km), and many Rwandans lived in homes and farms surrounding the park. They often wanted more farm and grazing land for their cattle. Villagers would ignore park rules and enter the park to collect firewood, honey, and sometimes water. Often, cattle of the local Watutsi farmers wandered into the park and destroyed plants that the gorillas ate.

Uncle Bert

Dian named Uncle Bert after a relative of hers—although her actual uncle did not consider this a compliment and never forgave her for doing so. When Dian first identified Uncle Bert, he was one of the young silverback gorillas in Group 4.

Uncle Bert loved to play. He'd lead the group's youngsters in a square dance type of game: "Loping from one tree to the next, each animal extended its arms to grab a trunk for a quick twirl before repeating the same maneuver with the next tree down the line." Then the gorillas would tumble down the hill; Uncle Bert led them back to the top, time and time again, for some more play among the trees.

At first Dian tried chasing the cows away. Then she began painting them with green spray paint. Finally, with a gun she kept in her cabin, she shot over their heads to scare them. Naturally, none of these methods pleased the farmers.

Even more than cattle, Dian hated the local poachers who set traps in the park to try to capture bushbucks and duikers, two small species of antelope. They depended on these antelope to provide food for their families. But the traps, with wire springs and a noose that would ensnare the animals' legs, would sometimes wrap around the hands and arms of gorillas who mistakenly stumbled into them. If the wire was not removed, the gorilla could lose a limb or die from an infection.

Dian believed poachers had to be stopped at all costs and became obsessed with daily trap searches. Given the number of poachers in the area and the number of staff at her disposal, she waged a losing battle. More snares existed than she could destroy.

On occasion, some poachers, following orders from park officials, seized young gorillas to sell. When Dian learned of one such capture, she personally complained to

Surrounded by her collection of gorilla bones and skulls, Dian records her observations.

Learning About Gorillas

A long with daily observation, Dian used the scientific tools of the time to find out more details about gorillas. She analyzed the bones and skulls she found in the area. Gorilla dung, also called spoor, provided all kinds of information about what the animals ate or what parasites and worms might be affecting their health.

Dian took careful notes about everything she learned. As she made new observations and discoveries, she sent messages to Louis Leakey to inform him of her findings.

the conservator of Volcanoes National Park, who intended to send the animal to the Cologne Zoo in Germany. But the official realized he could not properly care for the infant—named Coco—so he allowed Dian to bring her back to the camp. Coco was soon joined by a second baby gorilla also captured for the same purpose, Pucker.

Slowly Dian nurtured them back to health. She found the best way to feed them and the appropriate medications to keep them healthy. Then she did everything she could to make the young gorillas feel at home. She covered the cabin floors with nesting and feeding materials. She planted saplings in the cabin that could be used to climb to the ceiling. She basically turned her home into a mini rainforest and spent her days coddling the two.

When Coco got strong enough, she raided the food cabinet and sampled sugar, flour, jam, rice, and spaghetti before dumping them on

Dian walks with Coco and Pucker, who came to stay with her in 1969. Dian took a break from fieldwork to care for the two orphaned gorillas.

the floor. Both Coco and Pucker loved bananas; the fruit does not grow in the area, but they had been in captivity long enough to develop a taste for them. When they played outside, they would chase the camp chickens, and Coco loved to ride on the back of Cindy, Dian's pet boxer. The pair would run around in circles until they both collapsed, exhausted and dizzy.

Dian loved having the young gorillas in camp and kept delaying their transfer back to the park authorities. But Coco and Pucker had been promised to the zoo, and eventually, much to her dismay, they were flown to Cologne.

Whether working with gorillas like Coco and Pucker in her camp or those in the wild, Dian spent about two years simply focusing on these animals who delighted her so much. Apart from a few people in the area—camp workers, residents, and local officials—she had little interaction with humans. But given her breakthroughs in the study of gorilla behavior, her findings would inevitably catch the attention of those in the outside world. And that attention altered her life dramatically.

IN JANUARY 1970, DIAN PUBLISHED HER FIRST ARTICLE in *National Geographic.* In it, she began educating readers about the shy and peaceful nature of gorillas. Then in 1973, Robert Campbell's film appeared on television. In it were many scenes where Dian was close to and surrounded by gorillas, including the pivotal scene in which she and Peanuts touch hands. The program brought Dian's work to the attention of millions.

This international exposure brought many benefits. More worldwide recognition meant more money for her research center. Dian was able to fund a small village of cabins, a chicken house, and even a laundry. Soon graduate students came to live and work at Karisoke. Having

Dian stands in the doorway of her cabin at Karisoke. The cabin was made of green-painted metal.

Beethoven

Beethoven was the patriarch of Group 5—one of the gorilla groups Dian observed during her initial studies at Karisoke. The hulking male weighed around 400 pounds (181 kg). His silvery markings extended along his thighs, neck, and shoulders. An imposing figure, this gentle giant loved playing with his offspring. When Puck was a mere six months old, Beethoven would pick up the infant, dangle her, and groom her. Beethoven sired many children, and his position in the group was gradually transferred to his son Icarus.

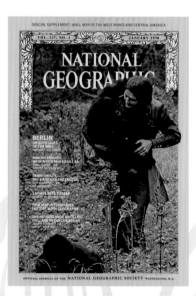

more hands meant she could do more accurate gorilla censuses and keep an eye on all the groups around her.

But Dian also paid a high price for her new-found fame. Since childhood, Dian had always been her best self while with animals. Now instead, she had to spend more time with people. Groups of tourists arrived, unannounced, because they had heard about her work. And directing students could be time-consuming and required diplomacy—not Dian's strength.

Intruders, all kinds of them, now invaded Dian's personal paradise. They often kept her from doing what she wanted to accomplish each day. She spent more time engaged in the business of running her research center than with her best friends—gorillas like Peanuts, Puck, and Digit. It became more and more difficult to find time to be alone in the wilderness.

A MOUNTAIN GORILLA'S DAY

A mountain gorilla spends about 40 percent of its day resting, 30 percent feeding, and 30 percent traveling in search of food. In a home range that measures 1.8 to 9 square miles (4.7–23 sq km), each family group spends days moving in search of the best available plants.

TRAVELING

Mountain gorillas rise with the sun, usually around six in the morning, year-round. They begin hunting for breakfast—fresh patches of thistles, nettles, or wild celery.

Unlike many primates, mountain gorillas spend most of their time on the ground. A mountain gorilla usually travels less than 0.6 mile (1 km) a day, but may travel farther for favorite foods.

Mountain gorillas eat both the leaves and shoots of the bamboo plant.

EATING

Mountain gorillas spend most of their daylight hours eating. As youngsters, they watch what their mother eats and pick up the remains of her food. They also learn to peel stems and search for dinner. Mountain gorillas are almost exclusively plant-eaters, feasting on more than 75 kinds of leaves, roots, and berries. Twice a year they feast on bamboo shoots, which grow during the two rainy seasons. These gorillas also spend time hunting for delicacies—mistletoe, pygeum tree fruit, and bracket fungus. On occasion, they might eat insects.

RESTING

By mid-morning, mountain gorillas rest as they digest their food, often belching and picking their teeth. Individuals may stop and groom one another. Others rest in the sunshine or make day nests, pulling plants together to form a mat. Then the cycle begins all over again: Feeding resumes until midday; they stop for a rest; then they forage, take another short rest, and hunt for more food.

Finally, right before the sun sets, the gorillas make new nests for sleeping. Constructed from bulky but nonedible plants, nests look like leafy, oval-shaped bathtubs. Mountain gorillas usually build nests on the ground, but other types of gorillas often build nests in trees. A young gorilla stays in its mother's nests until it is about three years old. Then it starts building its own nests.

A group of mountain gorillas rest on the slopes of Mount Karisimbi, the highest peak in the Virunga Mountains.

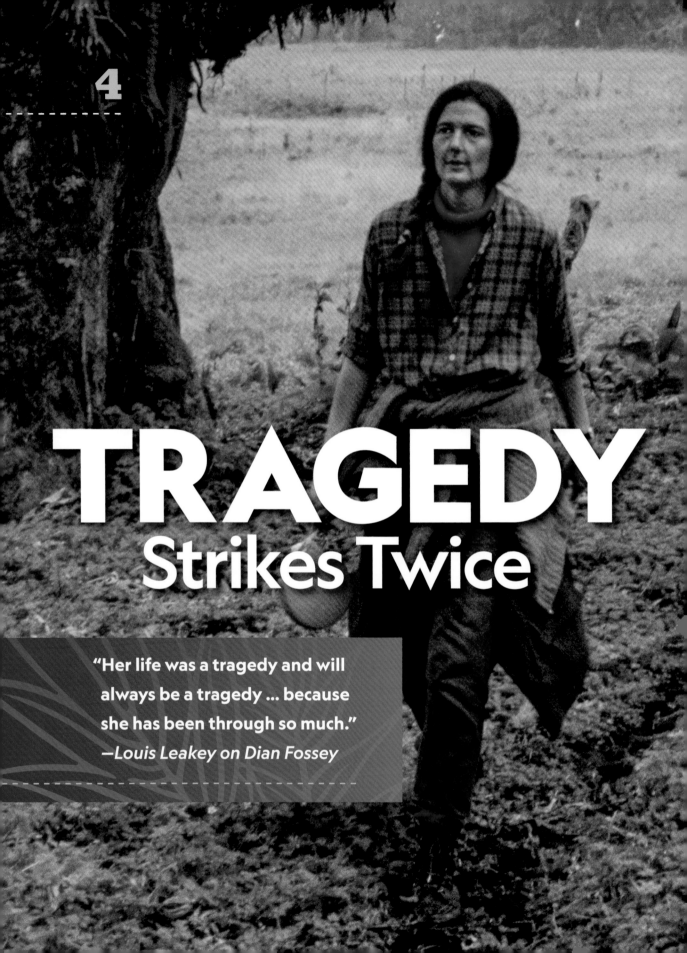

TRAGEDY
Strikes Twice

"Her life was a tragedy and will always be a tragedy ... because she has been through so much."
—Louis Leakey on Dian Fossey

Although dealing with fame and the increased population in camp annoyed Dian, the new threats to the safety of her gorillas worried her the most. The more humans looked at and observed gorillas, the more adapted to people the animals became. Hence, they were even more vulnerable to poachers.

Over time Dian escalated her activities against poachers, practicing what she called "active conservation." She began her efforts by hiring people to conduct antipoaching patrols. Then she tried to frighten poachers away by wearing scary masks and pretending she was a witch with magical powers.

- -

Dian walks in Volcanoes National Park, followed by park officials and cattlemen suspected of grazing cattle within the park's boundaries—a practice that disturbs gorillas and their habitat.

Eventually, Dian took the law into her own hands.
Rather than allowing local authorities to punish poachers, she started terrorizing them. She burned their prop-
erty, shot and killed their dogs. She even beat them with
stinging nettles. She went so far as to take a four-year-old child from one of the families
involved. Although the child was not harmed, the act was both unlawful and cruel.
Dian believed that she was doing the right thing: taking action to protect her beloved
gorillas from harm. But everyone else felt she had become too extreme. Even her closest
allies insisted she had no right to act the way she did. "I warned her," Jane Goodall said.
"Everyone who was fond of her did. But she didn't want to listen." Although her extreme
tactics deterred some poachers, most continued their activities.

ALTHOUGH DIAN ENJOYED INTERACTING WITH ALL THE GORILLAS, she had
developed the closest relationship with Digit. The young silverback gorilla became a
constant companion and would fall asleep next to her. At one point, Dian supplied
the government of Rwanda with a photo of Digit. Instead of being used to help protect
the gorillas from poachers, they placed it on a tourism poster that said: "Come and
see me in Rwanda."

On December 31, 1977, while Digit was defending his family from a group of poachers, he was killed. The poachers then cut off his head and hands to sell as trophies. When Dian learned of his death, she was overwhelmed with grief. Always quick to show her feelings, Dian had been "an emotional wreck" when Coco and Pucker left her camp. But Digit's death cut harder and deeper than anything else in her life. In her heart she had lost a close member of her family: "From that moment on, I came to live within an insulated part of myself."

After burying Digit in a patch of ground near her cabin, Dian sought revenge. As soon as the poachers were identified, they were arrested by the local government and spent time in prison for their actions. But Dian didn't stop there. She set out to publicize the story of Digit's death around the world. America's most famous evening news anchor, Walter

- - - - - - - - - - - - - - - - - -
When Dian found gorillas that had been killed by poachers—including her beloved Digit (*right*)—she created headstones for them and placed them in a graveyard near her cabin (*below*).

Cronkite of CBS, announced Digit's fate to the American public. Millions of his viewers knew the silverback gorilla because they had watched the National Geographic film that featured him. People around the world mourned the loss.

AROUND THIS TIME DIAN'S HEALTH BEGAN TO WORSEN. Living in the rainforest for so long and eating inadequately nutritional food, Dian grew increasingly sick from various ailments. Her list of problems over the years included being bitten by a spider, being attacked by her monkey Kima, and falling and breaking a rib. She also suffered from recurring pneumonia, an inflamed hip joint, hepatitis, and kidney infection.

Slowly, Dian began to exhibit the signs of alcoholism, the disease that had killed her father. Although some accounts of Dian abusing alcohol occurred before Digit's death, those who lived in camp started to notice her daily consumption of this drug after the

Facing Danger

Bustling with creatures big and small, the African rainforest is full of life—and deadly surprises. Dian had to learn to navigate wisely through the jungle, careful to avoid animal attacks, infectious diseases, and venomous scorpions and spiders. Despite her best efforts, Dian was surprised one day by an African buffalo charging at her. Realizing she was no match for the powerful, thousand-pound animal, Dian leaped quickly to get out of its way. She fell into a ditch and broke her ankle. Earlier in her studies, Dian came down with a high fever after being bitten by a dog. After consulting her medical book, she thought she might have rabies, so she left camp to get treatment.

African buffalo (*Syncerus caffer*)

tragedy. Porters would bring cases of alcohol to Dian's cabin;
all too soon, she sent them for more.

Dian's behavior became increasingly unpredictable.
By 1978, she rarely emerged from her cabin, not even for treks to be with the gorillas.
She spied on others in camp, opened their mail, and tape-recorded their conversations.
Two scientists at Karisoke called it "an asylum, with one very famous inmate in charge."

In all likelihood, her increased dependence on alcohol also led her to create
another set of enemies—people who might have otherwise been her allies. She started
to spar with students and the other scientists who lived in the area. Bill Weber and
Amy Vedder, former students of Dian, felt that a controlled ecotourism industry, with
limited permits allowed to visitors, could be helpful toward getting the government to
protect gorillas. They had brought in people who were trained in successful ecotourism practices by Biruté Mary Galdikas in Borneo. Officials in the Rwandan government
met the prospect of ecotourism with great enthusiasm. But Dian rallied against their
efforts. She believed that only virulent antipoaching activities made any sense.

Before returning to the United
States for a new job, Dian said
goodbye to the workers and friends
who helped her in Rwanda.

For several years, Dian's friends tried to convince her to go back to the United States and leave Karisoke in the hands of capable students she had trained. She had studied gorillas for more than a dozen years. Her friends assured her that she would be invaluable as a teacher for young graduate students. As one associate wrote her, "I also fear for your life ... that the herdsmen and poachers will try to get rid of you."

IN 1980, IN DESPERATE NEED OF MEDICAL ATTENTION, Dian finally agreed with her friends that a change of location would be good for her. She accepted an appointment as a visiting professor at Cornell University in New York State. While there, Dian's health improved and she seemed happier. Students admired her because she was a great storyteller and had a passion for her subject matter. While teaching, Dian finished writing *Gorillas in the Mist,* a book long in the making, which told the story of her experiences with mountain gorillas. During her productive tenure at Cornell, she also found time to team up, on three occasions, with the other two "Trimates," and lectured about what humans could learn from great apes. At these events, Dian made gorilla noises and Jane Goodall mimicked a chimpanzee pant-hoot—to the delight of all in attendance.

Gorillas in the Mist

Dian's 1983 autobiography, *Gorillas in the Mist,* tells her story and presents the discoveries she made about gorilla behavior. In it, Dian brings her gorilla friends to life. Dian even dedicated the book to some of her great ape muses: "To the memories of Digit, Uncle Bert, Macho, and Kweli." The book, a best seller when it was released, became even more widely recognized when the movie *Gorillas in the Mist* came out in 1988.

Some scenes in the movie show footage of real mountain gorillas in the wild. But it was dangerous for the actors to get too close to the gorillas. So the director worked with the crew to make lifelike gorilla suits. Actors studied the apes' posture and movements. The suits were so realistic—and the actors inside the suits were so convincing—that most people couldn't tell the difference.

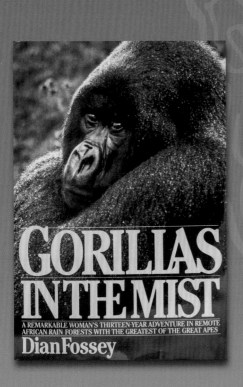

A gorilla portrait appears on the cover of Dian's autobiography (*left*), inspired by her 13 years studying the great apes.

The 1988 movie poster for *Gorillas in the Mist* (*above*) shows actress Sigourney Weaver with Digit, played by an actor in a gorilla suit.

Dian sits outside the
American Museum of Natural
History in New York City.

When *Gorillas in the Mist* was published, Dian embarked on a book tour, captivating audiences just as she did her students with her photographs and experiences. She even appeared on the popular television program *The Tonight Show*, hosted by Johnny Carson, entertaining him and the audience with her stories and gorilla sounds. The book was so successful that her publisher signed a deal for a Hollywood movie.

Dian—with her aging dog, Cindy—settled into life in America. Everyone hoped she would remain there—a famous woman scientist teaching the next generation of researchers. Clearly appreciated by her students, Dian was voted "Best Teacher."

Had Dian stayed in America, she might still be alive today. Both Jane Goodall, in her 80s, and Biruté Galdikas, in her 70s, continue to inspire, teach, and work on projects related to animal conservation and research. Dian could have followed that path, remaining in America to lecture and visiting her research station from time to time.

But she chose another fate.

EVEN WITH ALL THAT HAD HAPPENED AT KARISOKE, Dian still wanted to return permanently. By now, she needed an oxygen tank to make the climb to the camp. The Rwandan government did not welcome her. They refused to grant her more than short stays on her visa so that she continually had to leave camp, take a long trek into civilization, and beg for more time. Neither the current graduate students nor the other mountain gorilla researchers in the area seemed pleased she had returned.

But just before Christmas in 1985, she got what appeared to be a lucky break. Someone in the government decided to extend her stay for two years. Dian began to make plans in earnest to escalate her war against poachers.

Because Dian expected the movie crew that was making *Gorillas in the Mist* to arrive a couple days after Christmas, she delayed the holiday festivities so they could be filmed. As she always did, she decorated the entire camp "with

With money raised through the Digit Fund, Dian organized park guards into anti-poaching patrols.

candle-lit trees, garlands made from tinfoil, popcorn, and other homemade ornaments." She bought gifts for the staff and their families, wrapped them, and placed them under the trees.

But Dian had alienated far too many people—officials, local citizens, former and current students, and poachers. One or more of these individuals decided that they could not tolerate two more years of Dian Fossey living in Rwanda. Because she would not stay away, someone set out to kill her.

Poppy

Born on April 1, 1976, Poppy, daughter of Effie and Beethoven, was dubbed the "little darling" of Group 5 by Dian. Dian described her as "winsome and appealing" and said Poppy "could do no wrong." Full of personality, Poppy enjoyed sitting in the laps of human observers and loved being cuddled. Discarded bird nests particularly appealed to her; she beat them against the ground until only shreds remained.

In November 1985, Poppy left her group to live with another some distance away. But she came back 30 years later. Poppy became the oldest female observed giving birth, at the age of 41. Scientists believe Poppy passed away in 2019, after disappearing once more. She was the last living gorilla that Dian had studied.

Dian Fossey's grave is surrounded by the graves of gorillas she studied and loved.

On the night of December 26, 1985, after a long struggle with an intruder, Dian was murdered in her cabin.

When local authorities arrived, they touched and moved things, thus contaminating the crime scene. They also failed to gather all the available physical evidence. Later, they would try and convict two people for the murder—a former tracker and a graduate student who had been living in the camp. But none of her colleagues or friends felt these two were guilty. In a crime with few facts and little evidence, the list of possible suspects remains long to this day.

A few days after Dian's death, with the holiday decorations still hanging, grieving friends and staff buried Dian in the gorilla graveyard at Karisoke, beside her dear friend Digit. Diane could no longer protect her beloved mountain gorillas; fortunately for them, she had already inspired others to take up her mission.

THREATS AND CHALLENGES

Mountain gorillas are among the world's most critically endangered species. Today, just over 1,000 individuals exist in the wild. With help from park rangers and conservation programs, the population is on the rise. But the great apes face many threats that make survival a daily challenge.

POACHING

Snare traps, made of cables or wires, are set in the forest by poachers. The deadly traps are usually meant for other animals, such as antelope and bush-pigs, that wander through the forest. But the gorillas that share the forest with these animals also get caught in the traps, some-times getting injured or killed as a result.

Rangers keep an eye out for snares and other traps while on patrol for gorillas.

An infant gorilla lounges atop one of its family members.

HABITAT LOSS

Mountain gorillas once had much more room to roam. But over the years, huge patches of their forest home were cut down to make way for roads, farmland, and open spaces for livestock to graze. There is little habitat left for gorillas. Even protected areas, such as Rwanda's Volcanoes National Park, are under pressure from illegal activities such as woodcutting and water collecting by people living nearby.

Land cleared for farming borders Uganda's Bwindi Impenetrable Forest, which is also home to mountain gorillas.

Trackers with the Dian Fossey Gorilla Fund patrol the forest for signs of gorillas, as well as signs of danger.

WAR AND INSTABILITY

In the 1990s, a civil war broke out in Rwanda. The war, and the instability that followed, sent thousands of people over the border into the Democratic Republic of the Congo, where they lived on the edge of Virunga National Park, and poaching and deforestation increased. Today, Rwanda is considered one of the safest countries in Africa, and travelers come from around the world to catch a glimpse of gorillas. This tourism helps fund gorilla conservation. Unfortunately, conflicts continue on the other side of the Virunga Mountains in the DRC, endangering gorillas and the park rangers who work to protect them.

SAVING
the Gorillas
in the Mist

Every morning a large group of trackers wakes up in Rwanda around 5 a.m. They get breakfast and set out for an eight-to-nine-hour day to explore Volcanoes National Park. These employees of the Dian Fossey Gorilla Fund have a very serious mission—to protect and gather information about mountain gorillas.

Dian carries gorilla orphans Coco and Pucker through the forest.

67

"When you realize the value of all life, you dwell less on what is past and concentrate more on the preservation of the future."
—*Dian Fossey's last journal entry*

First, trackers locate gorillas' night nests and then follow clues, such as crushed vegetation or dung, that will lead them to the animals themselves.

Just like Dian once did, trackers check for health problems, changes in appearance, or additions or absences in the group. They search out and destroy poaching traps. Working alongside scientists, the trackers follow around 100 gorillas, who they know by name and personality, and make notes on their behavior.

All members of these teams have to be strong and smart. All need to understand the dangers of the forest—because some of their colleagues have lost their lives. But they have grown to love these gorillas and will do anything to protect them.

Both men and women serve on these teams and in every other capacity at Karisoke. Alphonsine Nakure, a mother of three children, farmed before she began tracking in 2008. She likes to talk about her favorite gorilla, Inkumbuza, a male silverback who has lived in two different gorilla groups. Nakure, who was once charged by a buffalo, has never been deterred by the rugged conditions of the landscape or by occasional dangers on the job. Pelagie Mutuyimana, who has a degree in wildlife management, heard stories about the gorillas when she was young and hoped that "one day I could help them through their conservation." Both women take extreme pride in their daily work.

A silverback mountain gorilla (*right*) shows dominance by beating his chest and making a loud call.

Pelagie Mutuyimana (*below*) is a tracker with the Dian Fossey Gorilla Fund. She helps protect endangered mountain gorillas.

BECAUSE OF DEDICATED INDIVIDUALS LIKE NAKURE, Mutuyimana, and many others in Rwanda who care about these incredible apes, the gorilla population has rebounded. In Dian's 1973 gorilla census, she recorded only 275 individuals living in and around Volcanoes National Park. But recently, scientists counted more than 600 animals. With more than two times as many of these magnificent creatures roaming the mountains than when Dian shared the area with them, mountain gorillas are hailed as one of the most successful conservation stories of our time.

Protecting the mountain gorilla population has taken legions of people. After Dian's death, different tactics needed to be adopted. Poachers had to be discouraged, sometimes even jailed. Local citizens became more involved in protecting the gorillas. Advocates needed to persuade local authorities to join in their efforts and find allies in government to aid their cause.

Cantsbee

Dian was sure that Cantsbee's mother, Puck, was a male gorilla—until she gave birth! When Dian saw the baby gorilla, born in 1978, she said, "It can't be!"

As an adult, Cantsbee led the largest group of gorillas ever observed. He held the longest reign of any silverback and, with 25 sons and daughters, fathered the most offspring. Nine of his sons are, or have been, dominant silverbacks, too.

One day, Cantsbee disappeared from his group, and was later found dead. He was the last dominant silverback that Dian ever studied. After Cantsbee died, his son Gicurasi took over leadership of the group.

Tourists spot a mountain gorilla in Volcanoes National Park. Money from tourism helps the park fund gorilla conservation.

In addition to physically monitoring the park, authorities had to establish appropriate ecotourism practices. The Rwandan government manages gorilla tourism and shares 10 percent of the park fees with local communities. The presence of tourists helps nearby businesses and creates jobs at local hotels and guesthouses.

BEFORE DIAN'S DEATH, TWO FINANCIAL FUNDS WERE ESTABLISHED THAT would prove to be critical to future conservation efforts. In 1978, because she did "not want Digit to have died in vain," Dian created the nonprofit Digit Fund to protect and monitor gorillas. This was later renamed the Dian Fossey Gorilla Fund in her honor. Shortly after Digit's death, famous naturalist and television broadcaster Sir David Attenborough arrived at Karisoke to film a segment of *Life on Earth* about the mountain gorillas.

Dian brought him to a gorilla family; they allowed him to lie next to them in the foliage and even snuggled him. Attenborough, so moved by the interaction, established the Mountain Gorilla Project to support the Rwanda parks department.

As a celebrity scientist, Dian managed to get media attention for the plight of the mountain gorillas. But her persuasiveness did not end with her death. Released in 1988, the film *Gorillas in the Mist*—with a riveting portrayal of Dian played by Sigourney Weaver—became an immediate commercial success and eventually a film classic. Generations of viewers found themselves entranced with gorillas, just as Dian had been.

While filming the movie *Gorillas in the Mist*, actress Sigourney Weaver (*left*) met some of the mountain gorillas from the groups Dian studied. Dian herself introduced Sir David Attenborough (*below*) to a gorilla family.

Gorilla Genetic Breakthroughs

In 2008, geneticists took a DNA sample from a western lowland gorilla who lived at the San Diego Zoo in California. At that point, they were able to get a full picture of the gorilla genome, which contains all the information about the makeup of these great apes.

With the new information, scientists learned a great deal about similarities and differences between gorilla and human DNA. So much of the human and gorilla genetic material is the same, but there are fascinating differences. For instance, gorillas have a gene that helps the skin on their knuckles grow a tough layer of keratin, hence they can more easily walk on them.

Genes are made up of DNA, which is packaged into threadlike structures called chromosomes (*above*).

Scientists working at Karisoke continued to face extreme challenges. In the 1990s, members of the Hutu, a Rwandan ethnic group, fought another group, the Tutsi, beginning a brutal civil war. In just 100 violent days, the Hutu killed 800,000 Tutsi, in what's known today as the Rwandan genocide against the Tutsi. During this time, Karisoke's location in the forest was destroyed, and operations were moved to a nearby town. But the mountain gorillas were not abandoned. The trackers continued protecting them, even at the risk of their own lives.

Today, many more techniques and technologies exist than Dian had at her disposal. Trackers using GPS units in the field can now precisely record gorilla movement patterns. Gorilla dung can be analyzed for viruses and parasites but also for DNA. It took Dian months or years to figure out the relationships between members of a family group; now DNA allows scientists to do this quickly.

These techniques have allowed scientists to learn more about gorilla behavior than ever before. Gorillas travel much farther from their own families than researchers

Scientist Gudula Nyirandayambaje collects data on mountain gorillas using a portable tablet.

realized. And although experts don't know much about how gorillas and other animals perceive death, recent observations have given scientists some insight. Gorillas have been observed as they gathered around and groomed their dead family members and gorillas from other families. Every discovery reveals that humans have yet to fully comprehend the complex emotional lives of mountain gorillas.

NO MATTER HOW CONTROVERSIAL OR AT TIMES MISGUIDED DIAN might have been, she succeeded in what she set out to do. In her own writing and in the films about her, she brought mountain gorillas to life for people and made them aware of the nuances, characteristics, and actions of individual gorillas. She convinced local authorities and other conservation groups about the ongoing importance of antipoaching efforts. Students trained in her program stayed in the area to aid the conservation efforts.

Koko

Arguably the world's most famous gorilla, Koko, a western lowland gorilla, was born July 4, 1971, at the San Francisco Zoo. As an infant, Koko was quite sickly, and Francine (Penny) Patterson, working on her doctorate at Stanford University, convinced the zoo to lend her the young gorilla for a sign language project that might take four or five years.

After bringing Koko to Stanford, Penny began teaching her American Sign Language (ASL). Her pupil progressed quickly: In 14 years, Koko learned to sign about 500 words. After 28 years, Koko had mastered around 1,000 words.

Before Koko's 12th birthday she used ASL to tell Penny that she wanted a cat as a present. Eventually one arrived, and Koko named her "All Ball." The two became inseparable. In 1985, Penny and Ronald H. Cohn, who photographed and filmed Koko all her life, published *Koko's Kitten,* a book that became a classroom favorite. With her ability to communicate with humans in sign language, Koko became a symbol of the amazing bond between gorillas and humans.

Koko the gorilla and scientist Penny Patterson share a moment with a kitten.

Our Endangered Cousins

All of the great apes—chimpanzees, bonobos, orangutans, and gorillas—share many characteristics with humans. They are highly intelligent and good at solving problems. Like humans, great apes usually have just one baby at a time, and they spend many years raising the baby. Sadly, all of the great apes are endangered.

Bonobos

Although similar to chimpanzees in many ways, bonobos live in groups that are usually led by a dominant female. These African apes live in the wild in forests of the Democratic Republic of the Congo.

Chimpanzees

Chimpanzees live in large groups led by dominant males in the forests of Central and West Africa. Jane Goodall observed chimpanzees using tools, something only humans were previously thought to do.

Orangutans

Orangutans are the only great apes found in Asia. They live on the islands of Borneo and Sumatra. Except for mothers and their young, orangutans mostly live alone. They spend almost all of their time in the trees.

Gorillas

Gorillas live in forests in West and Central Africa. They live in social groups led by a dominant male. As young gorillas grow up, they may stay in their birth group, or go off to join a new group.

Dian Fossey (*above*) made it her life's mission to study and protect mountain gorillas.

As Jane Goodall wrote, "There can be no doubt whatsoever that Dian did more to save the mountain gorillas than anyone."

"When I look at a gorilla, ... I'm looking at the better part of myself," Dian once said. As the years went on, Dian became remembered for the better part of herself—her long-term observation of gorillas and her cries for conservation of "the greatest of the great apes." She came to study them for a few months; she stayed for years. Her tombstone, which sits beside her gorilla friends, reminds us that she gave the ultimate sacrifice.

Dian Fossey
1932–1985
NO ONE LOVED GORILLAS MORE

REST IN PEACE, DEAR FRIEND

ETERNALLY PROTECTED

IN THIS SACRED GROUND

FOR YOU ARE HOME

WHERE YOU BELONG

DIAN'S LEGACY: THE DIAN

O riginally established by Dian in 1967, the Dian Fossey Gorilla Fund today works to conserve and protect gorillas and their habitats. It's the largest organization in the world fully dedicated to gorilla conservation. The Fossey Fund's staff protects gorilla families, studies how they live, and educates people about how they can help, too.

TRACKERS

W orking on the front lines, trackers monitor and support the gorilla population. The Fossey Fund supports dozens of trackers, who go through a rigorous selection and training process to make sure they have the skills and knowledge they'll need on the job.

Tracker Alphonsine Nakure *(right)* is one of the Fossey Fund's dedicated team members *(below)*.

FOSSEY GORILLA FUND

CONSERVATION AND EDUCATION

Each year, the Fossey Fund runs conservation and education programs for thousands of students. These programs train future scientists about gorillas, scientific methods, and how to conduct field research.

Tracker Pelagie Mutuyimana watches a group of gorillas and takes notes.

ADOPT A GORILLA

One way that people can directly support the Fossey Fund's critical conservation work is by symbolically adopting one of the animals the fund is working to protect. Through adoption, supporters can make a personal connection with a gorilla and learn more about its daily life. With each adoption, supporters get a certificate, photos and information about the gorilla, and a special video message.

Young gorillas such as Macibiri, seen here, can be symbolically adopted through the Fossey Fund.

FIELD NOTES
Resources and More

Tracker Leonard Nsengiyumva makes notes
on the mountain gorillas he's been following.

Where Eastern Gorillas Live

A F R I C A

Uganda

Democratic
Republic of
the Congo

Rwanda

AREA
ENLARGED
BELOW

There are two types of
eastern gorillas: mountain
gorillas and Grauer's
gorillas. Dian studied
mountain gorillas in the
Democratic Republic
of the Congo's Virunga
National Park and
Rwanda's Volcanoes
National Park, enlarged
at right.

Wild mountain
gorillas are found only
in Africa, in Rwanda,
the Democratic
Republic of the Congo,
and Uganda.

Central African Republic

South
Sudan

Ethiopia

Cameroon

Uganda

Congo

Kenya

Gabon

Democratic
Republic of
the Congo

Volcanoes
National Park

Rwanda

Burundi

Tanzania

Angola

**Where Eastern Gorilla
Subspecies Live**

Grauer's

Mountain

ATLANTIC
OCEAN

Zambia

Malawi

Mozambique

DEMOCRATIC REPUBLIC OF THE CONGO

UGANDA

Lake Mutanda

N

0 — 4 miles
0 — 4 kilometers

Mgahinga Gorilla National Park

Virunga National Park

Volcan Sabyinyo ▲

Volcan Gahinga ▲

▲ *Volcan Muhabura*

Volcanoes National Park

Lake Burera

Volcan Bisoke ▲

Karisoke Research Center ■

Volcan Karisimbi ▲

Lake Ruhondo

R W A N D A

Map Key
- ■ Point of interest
- ▲ Volcano
- Volcanoes National Park
- Other park or reserve

Lake Nyirakigugu

Buhanga Eco-Park

Lake Karago

Gishwati National Park

Gorilla Scrapbook

Titus

As a youngster, Titus lost his father (Uncle Bert) and his uncle (Digit) to poachers. Shortly after that, his mother fled the group, leaving Titus to fend for himself. Despite tragedy, this gentle-natured gorilla who Dian studied grew to be a legendary leader. In 2008, Titus was the subject of a BBC documentary called *Titus: The Gorilla King.*

Effie

Effie *(right),* part of Dian's Group 5, had nine sons and daughters. Effie's descendants became the largest wild mountain gorilla family ever recorded. The "Effie clan," as Dian and her team of researchers called the family, included daughters Puck and Maggie. Effie's grandsons Cantsbee, Isabukuru, and Mafunzo all went on to lead groups as silverbacks.

Puck

Puck was a dominant female in her group, which earned her special access to food and her pick of places to rest. After delivering Cantsbee, Puck went on to have seven more offspring. When Puck died, she was the oldest living member of the Effie clan.

Shinda

When Group 5 split in two, Shinda took the reins as leader of the new group. Though the silverback had a reputation of being tough and aggressive toward humans, the researchers who watched him grow up had a soft spot for him. When Shinda died, his group split into three, led by silverbacks Ugenda, Ntambara, and Urugamba.

Maggie

Maggie achieved star status during the filming of *Gorillas in the Mist*, when actress Sigourney Weaver declared Maggie was her favorite gorilla. Maggie's mother was Effie in Group 5, and her siblings included Puck, Tuck, and Poppy. When Maggie moved to a new group, she became the dominant female. After the leading silverback died fighting another silverback, Maggie kept the group safe for more than a month before merging with another group. Clever and cunning, she was also seen destroying snares set by poachers.

Macibiri

Granddaughter of legendary silverback Titus, youngster Macibiri was born in 2016. When she was an infant, she was very shy, often sticking close to her mother's side. As she got a little older, she got braver and more independent. There are no other gorillas her age in the group, so she looks to older gorillas—like Ndizeye and Segasira—during playtime, while her mother watches nearby.

Segasira

Born from Tuck, one of Effie's daughters, Segasira is a calm and happy gorilla—something he probably gets from his father, Titus. His name means "safeguard," or "protect." Segasira is strong, but small for a silverback. He loves to play with the youngsters of the group, but he is careful not to be too rough.

Itorero

In 2015, at the age of four, Itorero was caught in a snare trap. Veterinarians were able to remove the snare and Itorero recovered without permanent injuries. He was born to one of Effie's daughters, a dominant female named Mahane. Today, Itorero is very playful. His name refers to a traditional school where Rwandans study language, culture, and politics.

The Life of Dian Fossey: A Timeline

January 16, 1932
Dian is born in San Francisco, California, U.S.A.

1938
Dian's parents divorce.

1939
Dian's mother, Kitty, marries Richard Price.

1949
Dian graduates from high school and attends the University of California, Davis.

December 1966
Dian meets with National Geographic staff in Washington, D.C.; the Society funds her study on mountain gorillas.

January 1967
Dian sets up her first research camp in Kabara in the Democratic Republic of the Congo.

July 1967
Dian is forced to flee from the DRC after the military orders all foreigners out of the country.

1969
Dian cares for Coco and Pucker.

1970
Dian becomes the first human to hold hands with a gorilla, Peanuts.

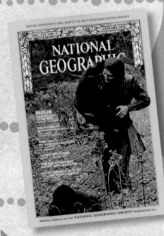

1970
Dian writes her first story for and appears on the cover of *National Geographic* magazine.

1983
Dian publishes her autobiography, *Gorillas in the Mist*.

1984
Dian returns to Karisoke.

December 26, 1985
Dian is murdered in her cabin at Karisoke.

December 31, 1985
Dian is buried in the gorilla cemetery at Karisoke.

1954
Dian graduates from San José State University with a degree in occupational therapy.

1955
Dian moves to Louisville, Kentucky, to work at Kosair Children's Hospital.

1963
Dian travels to Africa for seven weeks.

April 1966
Dian meets Louis Leakey in Louisville, Kentucky.

September 24, 1967
The Karisoke Research Center in Rwanda is founded.

1969
National Geographic sends photographer Bob Campbell to record Dian's work.

1970
Dian enrolls in a doctoral program in the University of Cambridge, England; she travels back and forth between England and Karisoke during her studies.

December 31, 1977
Digit is killed by poachers.

1978
Dian creates the Digit Fund, which is today known as the Dian Fossey Gorilla Fund.

1980
Dian lectures at Cornell University in Ithaca, New York, U.S.A.

1988
The film *Gorillas in the Mist* debuts in theaters.

2017
The Dian Fossey Gorilla Fund celebrates 50 years of helping people and saving gorillas.

2018
Mountain gorillas are moved from critically endangered to endangered status.

Key to Pictured Plants

Plants found in Volcanoes National Park, featured in illustrations throughout this book, are important resources for mountain gorillas and their habitat alike. With uses ranging from food to medicine to building materials, these Rwandan floras are both beautiful and useful. Although some plants are more prevalent than others, these featured examples are all essential to the park's thriving ecosystem.

Yushania alpina

This particular species of bamboo, which thrives in the park's volcanic soil, covers about 30 percent of the park. Gorillas, who eat the shoots and leaves, rely on bamboo as a key part of their diet. Bamboo also provides food for golden monkeys, and humans often use bamboo for construction, firewood, and handcrafts.

Hagenia abyssinica

Also known as the African redwood, this towering tree reaches up to 82 feet (25 m) tall and is very common within Volcanoes National Park. It has a thick trunk, shaggy flowers, and huge limbs adorned with moss, lichen, ferns, and orchids. Gorillas often settle themselves on a soft cushion of moss and pick out tidbits from the plant's branches to eat.

Lobelia wollastonii

Also known as giant lobelia, these flowering plants feature a woody stem, a cluster of leaves known as a rosette, and a shaggy flowering spike that can reach up to 23 feet (7 m). Although not a primary source of food for gorillas, giant lobelias can create safe spots for nests.

Neoboutonia macrocalyx

Neoboutonia macrocalyx, a type of evergreen tree, has large, broad, heart-shaped leaves. It grows in areas of high rainfall. In eastern Africa, the tree's wood is often used for firewood and building houses, and has a history of traditional medicinal use.

Sphagnum

Commonly called peat moss, this plant grows in wetlands throughout Volcanoes National Park. When this moss is submerged over millions of years, it breaks down into a thick, muddy, carbon-rich soil known as peat. When peat is harvested and dried, it can be used as a fuel for heating and electrical energy.

Dendrosenecio erici-rosenii

A member of the sunflower family, this plant features slim stems topped by leaf rosettes and yellow flowers, and can grow up to 30 feet (9 m) tall. The plant covers about 15 percent of Volcanoes National Park, where it provides food for herbivores like the bushbuck and black-fronted duiker.

Polystachya cultriformis

Polystachya cultriformis is one of the many varieties of orchid that grow throughout Rwanda and Volcanoes National Park. This particular species features small white or yellowish petals tinged in pink. The orchid is epiphytic, meaning that it grows on the surface of other plants. However, it does not harm its host. Instead, it gets its nutrients from moisture in the air or from decaying plant matter, which is a vital contribution to the local ecosystem.

Polystachya leonardiana

This beautiful orchid is one of 61 plant species found only in Rwanda. It stands out for its pink petals and purple stripes. Like many orchids, it is epiphytic, which means that it grows on the surface of other plants.

Further Resources

BOOKS

De la Bedoyere, Camilla. *No One Loved Gorillas More: Dian Fossey: Letters From the Mist.* Washington, D.C.: National Geographic, 2005.

Dakers, Diane. *Dian Fossey: Animal Rights Activist and Protector of Mountain Gorillas.* Crabtree Publishing Company, 2016.

Doak, Robin. *Dian Fossey: Friend to Africa's Gorillas.* Heinemann, 2014.

Fossey, Dian. *Gorillas in the Mist.* Boston: Houghton Mifflin, 1983.

Fowler, John. *A Forest in the Clouds: My Year Among the Mountain Gorillas in the Remote Enclave of Dian Fossey.* New York: Pegasus, 2018.

Goodall, Jane. *My Life With the Chimpanzees: The Fascinating Story of One of the World's Most Celebrated Naturalists.* New York: Simon & Schuster, 1988.

Matthews, Tom L. *Light Shining Through the Mist: A Photobiography of Dian Fossey.* Washington, D.C.: National Geographic, 1998.

Montgomery, Sy. *Walking With the Great Apes: Jane Goodall, Dian Fossey, Biruté Galdikas.* Boston: Houghton Mifflin, 1991.

Mowat, Farley. *Woman in the Mists: The Story of Dian Fossey and the Mountain Gorillas of Africa.* New York: Grand Central, 1988.

Ottaviani, Jim, and Maris Wicks. *Primates: The Fearless Science of Jane Goodall, Dian Fossey, and Biruté Galdikas.* New York: Square Fish, 2015.

Patterson, Francine. *Koko's Kitten.* New York: Scholastic, 1985.

Schaller, George B. *The Year of the Gorilla.* Chicago: University of Chicago Press, 1964.

Weber, Bill, and Amy Vedder. *In the Kingdom of Gorillas.* New York: Simon & Schuster, 2001.

ARTICLES

Fossey, D. "Making Friends With Mountain Gorillas." *National Geographic* 137, no. 1 (1970): 48–67.

Fossey, D. "More Years With Mountain Gorillas." *National Geographic* 140, no. 4 (1971): 574–85.

Fossey, D. "The Imperiled Mountain Gorilla: A Grim Struggle for Survival." *National Geographic* 159 (1981): 500–23.

Royte, Elizabeth. "The Gorillas Dian Fossey Saved Are Facing New Challenges." *National Geographic* 232 (2017): 111–27.

This mountain gorilla is a silverback named Mafunzo.

ONLINE

Discover more about mountain gorillas with National Geographic Kids: natgeokids.com/mountain-gorilla

Learn more about Dian and her groundbreaking foundation, the Dian Fossey Gorilla Fund: gorillafund.org

FILMS AND TELEVISION

Dian Fossey: Secrets in the Mist. National Geographic Channel, 2017.

Gorilla Family & Me. Directed by Susanna Handslip and David Johnson. BBC, 2015.

Gorillas in the Mist. Directed by Michael Apted. U.S.A.: Universal Pictures, 1988.

Mountain Gorillas' Survival: Dian Fossey's Legacy Lives On. Produced by Craghoppers. National Geographic Short Film Showcase: video.nationalgeographic.com/video/short-film-showcase/00000148-d73c-d457-a968-dfbde6c90000.

Titus: The Gorilla King. Directed by David Allen. Tigress Productions, 2008.

Virunga. Directed by Orlando von Einsiedel. U.S.A.: Netflix, 2014.

Notes

Chapter 1: Drawn to Gorillas

14 "Even as an adult, Dian loathed ..." Sy Montgomery, *Walking With the Great Apes*, 41.

14 "Knowing she did not measure up ..." Bill Weber and Amy Vedder, *In the Kingdom of Gorillas*, 237.

16 "a tremendous amount of care ..." Farley Mowat, *Woman in the Mists*, 3.

16 "marvelous sense of humor ..." Camilla de la Bedoyere, *No One Loved Gorillas More*, 6.

18 "in a dappled half-light ..." Camilla de la Bedoyere, *No One Loved Gorillas More*, 26.

18 "beautiful creatures with thick ..." Camilla de la Bedoyere, *No One Loved Gorillas More*, 26.

19 "Leakey had always preferred ..." Jane Goodall, *My Life With the Chimpanzees*, 48.

19 "virtually memorizing ..." Dian Fossey, *Gorillas in the Mist*, 4.

Chapter 2: A Mission in the Mountains

24 "Neither destiny nor fate ..." Farley Mowat, *Woman in the Mists*, 1.

28 "He was my last link ..." Dian Fossey, *Gorillas in the Mist*, 7.

31 "musky-barnyard, humanlike ..." Dian Fossey, *Gorillas in the Mist*, 3.

31 "walk on her knuckles ..." Dian Fossey, *Gorillas in the Mist*, 13.

31 "learned how to identify individual gorillas ..." Dian Fossey, *Gorillas in the Mist*, 11.

32 "cans of hot dogs ..." Dian Fossey, *Gorillas in the Mist*, 9.

32 "I never fully realized ..." Farley Mowat, *Woman in the Mists*, 41.

32 "everything is fairly jumbled ..." Camilla de la Bedoyere, *No One Loved Gorillas More*, 44.

35 "If people like you and me ..." Sy Montgomery, *Walking With the Great Apes*, 117.

Chapter 3: Befriending the Greatest of the Great Apes

39 "The more you learn ..." Los Angeles Times Wire Service, December 29, 1985. latimes.com/archives/la-xpm-1985-12-29-mn-25922-story.html

40 "They look like they are floating ..." Farley Mowat, *Woman in the Mists*, 289.

40 "sounds of wildlife all around ..." Dian Fossey, *Gorillas in the Mist*, 125.

42 "Dian marveled at how gentle ..." Dian Fossey, *Gorillas in the Mist*, 64.

42 "Their songs sounded like ..." Sy Montgomery, *Walking With the Great Apes*, 125.

43 "explosive, half-screaming sound ..." George Schaller, *The Year of the Gorilla*, 14.

43 "the first time she felt afraid ..." Dian Fossey, *Gorillas in the Mist*, 55.

43 "I've finally been accepted ..." Dian Fossey, *Gorillas in the Mist*, 141.

44 "Offered a *National Geographic* ..." Dian Fossey, *Gorillas in the Mist*, 80–81.

44 "He often invited play ..." Camilla de la Bedoyere, *No One Loved Gorillas More*, 80.

44 "a big toothy grin ..." Dian Fossey, *Gorillas in the Mist*, 172.

46 "If the wire ..." John Fowler, *A Forest in the Clouds*, 83.

47 "When they played outside ..." Dian Fossey, *Gorillas in the Mist*, 116.

Chapter 4: Tragedy Strikes Twice

52 "Her life was a tragedy ..." Sy Montgomery, *Walking With the Great Apes*, 73.

54 "I warned her ..." Sy Montgomery, *Walking With the Great Apes*, 186.

55 "an emotional wreck ..." Sy Montgomery, *Walking With the Great Apes*, 72.

55 "From that moment on ..." Dian Fossey, *Gorillas in the Mist*, 206.

57 "Dian's behavior became increasingly ..." Bill Weber and Amy Vedder, *In the Kingdom of Gorillas*, 239–240.

57 "an asylum, with one ..." Bill Weber and Amy Vedder, *In the Kingdom of Gorillas*, 245.

58 "I also fear for your life ..." Farley Mowat, *Woman in the Mists*, 152.

62 "candle-lit trees, garlands ..." Dian Fossey, *Gorillas in the Mist*, 166.

Chapter 5: Saving the Gorillas in the Mist

67 "When you realize the value ..." Farley Mowat, *Woman in the Mists*, 365.

71 "not want Digit ..." Dian Fossey, *Gorillas in the Mist*, 207.

77 "There can be no doubt ..." Diane Dakers, *Dian Fossey*, 102.

77 "When I look at a gorilla ..." Robin Doak, *Dian Fossey*, 42.

84 Gorilla Scrapbook adapted from profiles provided by the Dian Fossey Gorilla Fund

Index

Boldface indicates illustrations.

Index

Photo Credits

Endnote

Tara Stoinski observing Titus in Volcanoes National Park

Gorillas are amazing. Like us, they form lifelong relationships, look after their most vulnerable, laugh and even sometimes sing when they are happy, and mourn their dead. That's not surprising, given that they share more than 98 percent of our DNA. But prior to Dian Fossey's pioneering work, we knew none of this. One of Dian's lasting legacies is changing our perception of gorillas from ferocious beast to gentle giant, which inspired generations after her to care about the great apes and their future. Another legacy is the organization she started—renamed in her honor after her death—which is now the world's largest and longest-running organization dedicated to gorilla conservation. The Dian Fossey Gorilla Fund is extremely proud to have helped bring mountain gorillas back from the brink of extinction, but we still have much work to do. Sadly, gorillas still face many threats to their existence. That is why we are steadfast in our mission to protect individual gorillas and their families, to conduct the cutting-edge science that underlies conservation strategies, to train the next generation of conservation leaders, and to help improve the lives of people who share the gorillas' forest home. For gorilla conservation to succeed, it will take all of us working together. And the great news is that by saving gorillas, we ultimately save ourselves. Gorillas are the gardeners of the second largest tropical rainforest remaining on Earth—the literal lungs of the planet and one of our best natural defenses against climate change.

Dian Fossey taught us the power we each have to make a difference. Now it is our job to ensure that mountain gorillas have a future. By reading this book, I hope you have been inspired, as I was more than 30 years ago when I first learned about Dian Fossey, to be the change you want to see in the world. That is perhaps Dian's biggest legacy of all.

Tara Stoinski, Ph.D.
President, CEO, and Chief Scientific Officer
Dian Fossey Gorilla Fund

Author's Note

After writing books about Jane Goodall (*Untamed)* and Biruté Galdikas (*Undaunted)*, two of the three "ape ladies" mentored by Louis Leakey, I embarked on this biography of Dian Fossey. Although I knew that she would test my skills as a researcher, I had no idea how much.

As someone who always focuses on primary sources, I intended to rely on Dian's book *Gorillas in the Mist,* her letters, and the numerous print and video interviews she gave while alive. But only slowly did I realize that she would prove to be an unreliable narrator about her own life.

In fiction, an unreliable narrator can create exciting tension for readers, just as Holden Caulfield does in *The Catcher in the Rye*. These characters tell fascinating stories but cannot be trusted because they don't bother telling the truth. But nonfiction writers embrace truth-telling.

Dian Fossey rarely let a fact get in the way of a good yarn. Consequently, I had to check much of what she wrote or said against other sources. Sometimes the decisions about what I could include were easy. For instance, Dian's rendition of her meeting with Louis Leakey in Louisville matched in tone and feeling the accounts by both Jane Goodall and Biruté Galdikas of their sessions with Leakey. Because of that, I decided I could include her version. But when she fled her first research camp, she told so many variants of the story that I had no way to determine what actually happened; hence, I only summarized the essence of her journey, leaving out most of the details. Fortunately, Tara Stoinski, president, CEO, and chief scientific officer for the Dian Fossey Gorilla Fund, painstakingly reviewed the manuscript. I am particularly grateful for her assistance. Biologist and conservationist Ian Redmond, OBE, helped improve the final pages with his insightful comments.

The author's name appears on the cover of a book, but in fact, it contains the work of many people. I was aided and abetted in the editorial process by the brilliant Kate Hale, to whom this book is dedicated. A devoted nonfiction editor, she exemplifies the Mies van der Rohe's statement "God is in the details." Erica Green gave the project a fresh reading and provided insightful editorial comments. Then Marfé Ferguson Delano, with a steady hand and an eye toward deadlines, moved the project to a finished book. Team *Unforgotten* also worked their magic: award-winning designer Marty Ittner; Amanda Larsen, design director; Sarah J. Mock, senior photo editor; Rose Davidson, photo caption and sidebar researcher; Ebonye Gussine Wilkins, sensitivity reviewer; Alix Inchausti, production editor; Mike McNey, cartographer; and Anne LeongSon and Gus Tello, design production assistants. It truly took a village to make *Unforgotten* as visually exciting as it is.

Many years ago I interviewed celebrities for *Everything I Need to Know I Learned From a Children's Book*. In the process I found out that about a third of them actually chose careers based on a book they encountered in childhood. With that in mind, I have presented to my readers a trilogy about three women who changed our understanding of the animal world as they spent their lives protecting chimpanzees, orangutans, and mountain gorillas. I can only hope their devotion and passion pass on to the next generation. —Anita Silvey